WOMEN IN SCIENCE

Dorothy Hodgkin

Biochemist and Developer of Protein Crystallography

Cavendish Square

New York

Kristin Thiel

Published in 2017 by Cavendish Square Publishing, LLC
243 5th Avenue, Suite 136, New York, NY 10016

Library of Congress Cataloging-in-Publication Data
Names: Thiel, Kristin.
Title: Dorothy Hodgkin: biochemist and developer of protein crystallography / Kristin Thiel.
Description: New York : Cavendish Square, 2017. | Series: Women in science | Includes index.
Identifiers: ISBN 9781502623133 (library bound) | ISBN 9781502623140 (ebook)
Subjects: LCSH: Hodgkin, Dorothy, 1910-1994--Juvenile literature. | Crystallographers--Great Britain-
-Biography--Juvenile literature. | Scientists--Great Britain--Biography--Juvenile literature.
Classification: LCC QD903.6.H63 T45 2017 | DDC 548'.09--dc23

1 7/02

Editorial Director: David McNamara
Editor: Leah Tallon/Kristen Susienka
Copy Editor: Rebecca Rohan
Associate Art Director: Amy Greenan
Designer: Alan Sliwinski
Production Coordinator: Karol Szymczuk
Photo Research: J8 Media

Printed in the United States of America

CONTENTS

The lab was Dorothy Hodgkin's
home away from home.

INTRODUCTION

A MAJOR PRESENCE IN THE STUDY OF TINY MATTER

I n 1964, not even four out of every one hundred women had completed four years of college. About seven out of one hundred people working in science, technology, engineering, and mathematics were women. That year, Dorothy Crowfoot Hodgkin won the Nobel Prize in **Chemistry** for her work in **crystallography**. The Nobel Prize is considered one of the world's highest achievement awards in chemistry. Hodgkin was the third woman to win the Nobel Prize in Chemistry and remains one of only four women ever to win it.

WHAT IS CRYSTALLOGRAPHY?

Hodgkin used crystallography as a chemist. Crystallography is the study of the **atomic structures** and **molecular structures** of everything from proteins and viruses to glass and fiber—and even gases. It is the study of a thing's basic, foundational makeup. It is **cross-disciplinary**, meaning many fields of study use it. Chemistry, geology, biology, and physics are some of those fields that benefit from crystallography's approach.

Hodgkin was a leader in the technique of **X-ray crystallography**, which uses beams of strong, invisible light to see inside things. Because of the advances she and other scientists made in crystallography, today we are able to learn much more, much faster, than we could before.

Crystallography has an interesting history when it comes to women. Traditionally, and still today, there are more men than women studying and being recognized for their work in the sciences. The science of crystallography, a branch of natural science, has been no exception. But it has seemed to attract and encourage more women than other physical sciences. Hodgkin was but one pioneering female crystallographer.

By knowing what something is made of—its atomic structure—we learn how it functions. Knowing how something operates allows us to work with it. The pharmaceutical and biochemical fields rely a lot on crystallography to understand diseases and cells and then to make better medicines. Hodgkin contributed to health by determining what makes up penicillin, insulin, and vitamin B12.

WHO WAS DOROTHY HODGKIN?

Born in 1910 in Egypt to British parents, Dorothy Hodgkin attended school in England. She studied chemistry from a very young age, and as she grew up, she never wavered in her commitment to science, even when she married. In fact, she earned her doctorate, the highest degree possible in her field, in 1937, the same year she married. Her career began as her family did. Most of her important work in chemistry happened as she raised three children.

Hodgkin is most known for being a groundbreaking scientist, but she was also passionate about promoting world peace and safety for scientists doing work in dangerous places. For more than a decade, she led the Pugwash movement, which was concerned with people using scientific research for good purposes, to help everyone rather than hurt anyone.

Hodgkin died in 1994, but her discoveries remain useful today, and people still work toward her social values. Many of the students she taught went on to make their own important discoveries, and many more use the technique she helped to develop. One hundred years after her birth, fifty-six thousand atomic structures had been calculated using crystallography.

Other discoveries, some beyond our imagination, are sure to follow. Hodgkin herself suggested that one of the most important things her work offered was possibility. X-ray crystallography can answer questions we know we have and questions we haven't even thought of yet. In her Nobel Prize lecture, she said, "A great advantage of X-ray analysis … is its power to show some totally unexpected and surprising structure with … complete certainty."

London, the United Kingdom's capital and its most populated city, has always bustled with activity, even before multilane roads, skyscrapers, and power lunches. This photo was taken in 1922, when Hodgkin was twelve years old.

FROM CLASSROOM TO LABORATORY: ALWAYS DOROTHY

Dorothy Hodgkin lived at a time when it was not common for women to be scientists, or to have much of an education at all. However, during her life she not only excelled at school but also went on to complete her PhD, or doctorate. Though she earned the right to shout her qualifications from the mountaintop, she did not. For the most part, she was a simple, humble person. She asked even her newest and youngest coworkers to call her by her first name.

STARK DIFFERENCES IN CHILDHOODS

When she went into labor with Dorothy, her first child, on May 12, 1910, Grace (known as Molly) Crowfoot was far from her home country of England. She was in Cairo, Egypt, because her husband, John Crowfoot, worked for the Egyptian Education Service. Grace's work was also focused in the Middle East and northern Africa. She was an authority in early weaving techniques and was a botanical artist—she drew the plants of the region. When they lived in Sudan, young Dorothy often would walk with her mother to collect flowers.

Hodgkin, the Crowfoots' firstborn, grew up in a special situation. Her parents were educated and had good jobs that allowed the family to live in interesting places and learn a lot. In addition to her own intelligence and determination, Hodgkin could credit her parents and sheer good luck for helping her rise to greatness in science, humanitarian work, and family life.

Many other people at that time faced work and life challenges. Even for boys and men, the world in the early to mid-1900s could be a difficult place. In the United States, child labor wasn't made illegal until 1938. Work was difficult, tiring, and often dangerous. The 1911 Triangle Shirtwaist Factory Fire was a terrifying example of what could go wrong in modern industrial society. People received low wages for working long hours in the unsanitary and dangerous Triangle Shirtwaist Factory. When a fire broke out, many workers could not escape because the exits were locked, the fire escapes could not support the weight of the people, and the firefighters' ladders and hoses could not reach high enough. Most of the 146 people who died were in their teens or twenties, some as young as fourteen years old.

In 1917, the United States entered World War I, and the Selective Service Act, passed on May 18, 1917, introduced the draft. This meant the military could order men between the ages of twenty and thirty to join the military and go to war. Also at this time in the United States, there was great racial injustice and unrest. Lynchings were legal, race riots happened with some frequency, and the Ku Klux Klan operated in most of the states.

For everyone, education was a luxury. In 1910, there were as many people twenty-five years or older who had less than an eighth-grade education as there were people with more than an eighth-grade education. Fewer than four out of every one hundred women had completed four years of college. Almost one-third (30.5 percent) of those identifying as "black and other" in the US Census were illiterate, unable to read or write in any language. Five percent of whites were illiterate.

Hodgkin had a different experience. Her science education began around age ten, when her mother took her to an exhibition on **geology** at Gordon College in Sudan, where guides instructed on panning for gold. Excited by this idea of studying rocks and dirt, young Hodgkin repurposed a dish from her parents' kitchen to do her own sifting through sand, dirt, and rock in the stream that ran through her backyard. While many children may have stopped at that point, Hodgkin took her finds back to the college. She had a **hypothesis** about what she'd found, and she wanted to run tests to confirm this educated guess. What she found surprised her: ilmenite. This mineral made of iron and titanium wasn't mentioned in her textbooks. (It is found on the moon! And, interestingly, geology also studies the rocks of other places like the moon.) Fortunately, the Sudanese government's chemist, A. F. Joseph, was also a family friend. He helped her solve that puzzle and set up her own home laboratory. She bought glass tubes and crystals from the chemist. Later, when interviewed for the story preservation website Web of Stories, Hodgkin would laugh when she remembered how funny it was that he "didn't seem to have any particular rules about what he shouldn't … allow ten-year-old children to have."

SCHOOL DAYS

When World War I broke out, Molly Crowfoot took her four daughters to England for safety. She didn't stay long. Work—hers and her husbands—called from Africa. The family would reunite in England only a few months every year. At that time, it was not uncommon for families who worked in jobs like the Crowfoots' to live in separate countries.

Now living across the world from her parents, young Dorothy Hodgkin continued to excel in science, conducting exciting experiments. She was one of two girls allowed to join the boys in chemistry class—which was taught by a woman. "If a girl was going to a university, or hoped to go to a university, she could do chemistry, and I think that I know several girls who were persuaded by [that teacher] to do chemistry," Hodgkin said in a Web of Stories interview decades later. In one lesson, the students mixed a solution of alum and copper sulfate. Crystals grew from the solution over the next few days. This was Hodgkin's first exposure to what she'd learn was crystallography. That type of science gathers data from a pure form of a substance, a crystal. Crystals are often thought of as jewels or as beautiful stones found in caves. But many substances can be crystallized. You can grow crystals of a substance. In a crystallized sample of a substance, all the molecules are arranged in a regular, orderly pattern across all three dimensions.

COLLEGE DAYS

Before Hodgkin's college classes started, she went on an archaeological dig with her parents at Jerash, in Jordan. After working for the education service, her father became the director of education and antiquities in Sudan, which is the country immediately to the south of Egypt, and then the director of the British School of Archaeology in Jerusalem,

A KIDS' BOOK MAKES AN IMPRESSION

When Hodgkin won the Nobel Prize for Chemistry in 1964, she had been in her profession for about thirty years. During her career, she had studied and worked with a lot of important people, but the person she named in the first sentence of her Nobel Lecture, W. H. Bragg, was an influence from her childhood.

Bragg also won a Nobel Prize, in 1915. Even though he won in physics, not in chemistry, his work was similar to Hodgkin's. He won the award for using X-rays to analyze the structures of things. Hodgkin's mother gave her Bragg's children's book, *Concerning the Nature of Things* (1925),

MR. W. H. BRAGG
Trinity College, Third Wrangler

when Hodgkin was fifteen. This book told its young audience about scientists using X-rays to "see" inside things, to see their atomic structures. Hodgkin said in her Nobel Prize lecture that she first learned about X-rays and structures from that book.

With detailed paintings, Hodgkin recorded the mosaics uncovered during her and her parents' time in Jerash, Jordan.

Israel. He led several archaeological digs in the Middle East. His oldest daughter's job was to record the patterns of the mosaics on the remains of more than a dozen fifth- and sixth-century Byzantine churches that they uncovered, in order to help them learn about the people who used to live there. She never wavered from her commitment to science, but as she worked alongside her parents to excavate the site, she realized she wasn't sure which science she wished to study.

Hodgkin started studying archaeology and chemistry in 1928, her first year at Somerville College, one of the women's colleges at Oxford University. Oxford is made up of colleges; when you attend Oxford, you are a student of both Oxford and a particular college. Those colleges used to be single-sex, some admitting only women and some only men. Hodgkin analyzed glass tiles, also called tesserae, from the Jerash site with E. G. J. Hartley, an Oxford chemist. She told her parents about it in a letter in 1929. She was most excited about finding a small, or trace, amount of titanium in the blue glass. Finding the metal reminded her of one of her first experiments back when she was about fourteen. Together with Dr. Joseph in Sudan, she had tested for titanium and found it. She had kept her notes, and they'd proven useful to her as an adult.

As part of her chemistry degree, she took a course in crystallography. Impressed with her work, her tutor, F. M. Brewer, suggested she do research using X-ray crystallography. Now Hodgkin wouldn't be growing crystals and laboriously trying to study through experimentation what was happening in them. She'd be seeing inside them with X-ray technology.

When you think of X-rays, you probably think of being able to see inside the body. That is what Hodgkin was going to do: see inside crystallized versions of substances by using X-rays.

Her first project was thallium dialkyl halides with H. M. Powell, another chemist working out of the university. Hodgkin was happy with the strong crystals she grew and her drawings of them, even though their equipment led to some blurry photographs. Step by step, she progressed toward her ultimate field of work.

One of her favorite visiting lecturers at Oxford, a man by the name of J. D. Bernal, taught regularly at Cambridge, and Dorothy Crowfoot had her eye on working with him. It didn't hurt that she was fed up with Oxford's equipment. She reminisced later, laughing, that the **X-ray tube** at Oxford was so moody—sometimes working and sometimes not—that she might as well see another lab. Dr. Joseph, her childhood neighbor and the man who'd helped her with her first lab, played a role in introducing her and Bernal. Hodgkin soon went to Cambridge and found herself studying with Bernal, whose work on sterols she thought "very revolutionary." Bernal also immediately appreciated Hodgkin's natural way with X-ray crystallography, including her ease making thousands of complex mathematical calculations to create a **Patterson map**, a contour map that could be used to define the distances between **atoms** in a crystal. Along with working together, the two formed a brief romantic relationship, although it would end amicably several years later.

Together, Bernal and Hodgkin photographed with X-rays the single crystals of the protein pepsin, launching **protein crystallography** in 1934. Protein had never before been photographed in this way.

In the middle of the experimentation, when she was twenty-four years old, Hodgkin was diagnosed with **rheumatoid arthritis**, a disease causing joint pain. It would last her whole life. She was advised to take a break, but she refused. The secrets of pepsin were within sight! Besides, summer was around the corner—she would rest when everyone else did. Hodgkin recognized an exciting project when she saw one, and it was smart that she didn't take a break in the middle of the pepsin project. X-ray crystallography offered a leap in scientific experimentation, and proteins such as pepsin offered a marvelous puzzle that put crystallography to the test.

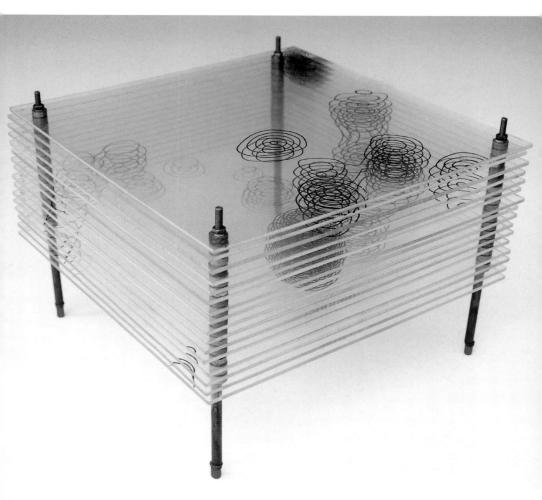

This three-dimensional map shows penicillin's electron density and position of individual atoms.

Proteins are large, complicated biological molecules. When they're hard at work, protein strands fold over on themselves into tangles. To understand how that can make scientific research complicated, consider this: Is it easier to photograph an entire piece of rope if it's stretched out or if it's tied in a knot? If you want to see what a person looks like,

Though Hodgkin eventually used early computers, most of her computing and mapping of atoms was done by hand.

would you ask for a photo of that person standing straight or curled up? Scientists don't learn all they need to if they take the "easy" photo, of the protein when it's a strand. They have to photograph the folded-over protein in order to see how it works, because it's only working when it's folded over.

The fact that Bernal and Hodgkin were able to take a photograph of pepsin that clearly showed its complicated structure is impressive on its own merits. But this was not purely an academic pursuit; Bernal and Hodgkin didn't do this just to see if they could. There were practical applications. They learned that protein molecules are unique from all other types of molecules. Unlocking the secrets of pepsin opened the door to understanding insulin, hemoglobin, and viruses, which later would lead to major advancements in health and medicine. Hodgkin and Bernal's experiment with pepsin also helped them advance X-ray crystallography's process. Until their work, crystals were taken out of their **mother liquor**, the solution left over after crystallization, before they were studied. Bernal found the pepsin crystals, left in the air, were too shriveled to photograph. Keeping them in liquid, a new tactic, made this success possible.

CHANGING THE WORLD OUTSIDE THE LAB

Bettering the community was always as important to Hodgkin as making discoveries in the lab. She desired peace and freedom of education around the world, even in countries that her home country of England considered enemies, such as the Soviet Union, China, and North Vietnam. She so wanted the research of scientists in other countries to succeed that she supported them in deed as well as in word.

Chinese researchers were studying the insulin structure at the same time Hodgkin was, and she visited them more than once to compare notes.

Hodgkin's mother was her first example that one should work for good. Molly Crowfoot took her fifteen-year-old daughter to the Sixth Assembly of the League of Nations, which focused on international disagreements being sorted out through debate, not wars. Another strong influence on Hodgkin, especially in adulthood, was one of the first people she met at college. Margery Fry, principal of Somerville College, was also a social activist who was influential in prison reform and victim compensation. Later, Hodgkin would become close friends and colleagues with Bernal, who, besides being her academic advisor, was very politically active. And the man Hodgkin would live most of her adult life with, her husband, shared many beliefs with her.

Fry introduced the two while they both were staying at her house in London. Thomas Hodgkin had been working for the British government in Palestine. During the Arab revolt of 1936–1939, he visited Jewish and Arab prisoners alike and was so affected by what he saw that he resigned. Eventually, he found himself back in England. When his future wife met him, he was applying to teach grammar school. As she reflected later, thankfully for everyone involved, since he was not good with discipline, he took a job in young adult education. Specifically, he worked within his passion for service work—he taught unemployed minors.

Hodgkin started her life with an excellent foundation of support from her extensive network of family and friends. From them she learned to be both curious about the world and compassionate with her work. She was never a wallflower in this regard, but she really came into her own in college, when she was a young adult ready to put what she was learning into practice.

Dorothy Hodgkin, age seventy-nine

CHAPTER TWO

A LAB OF HER OWN

After two years at Cambridge, Hodgkin returned to Oxford in 1934 with a fellowship from Somerville. She was well invested in chemistry, crystallography, X-ray diffraction, and X-ray crystallography, and was committed to exploring what each could do. As a study of atomic and molecular structures, crystallography works well with many different sciences, but Hodgkin used it from a chemist's perspective. When an X-ray hits a crystal, it diffracts—or shoots off in different directions, bouncing off the atoms in the crystal—and the result of this is X-ray crystallography.

As Hodgkin continued to work, she continued living her dreams, proving the stuff of her imagination with math and experimentation. Crystallography may not seem like a science that's easy to visualize because what the researchers study is too small to see or touch, but there actually are a lot of moments you can picture.

HODGKIN'S NEW HOME

When we think of laboratories today, we may envision sterile rooms in blocky buildings built only for function. Hodgkin's was in the Oxford Museum, a Victorian neo-Gothic beauty full of meaning. Influenced by art critic John Ruskin, who liked the idea of nature influencing architecture, it was perfect for housing a lab that studied the very essence of naturally occurring substances. For example, wrought-iron pieces twisted in archways to look like sycamore, walnut, and palm tree branches. Each column in the courtyard was made of a different rock found in Britain. Statues of scientists such as astronomer Galileo and evolutionary theorist Charles Darwin may have appeared to look on as Hodgkin and her students worked.

Her lab was tucked into a corner of this building. On a sunny day, a little light must have filtered through the one ornate window with its pointed arch. Using a ladder—there were no stairs—Hodgkin and her students accessed the gallery where the X-ray machine sat. Hodgkin also worked as a chemistry tutor at Somerville, so her students were seniors at Somerville and people from a variety of Oxford colleges completing their PhDs. They were following tradition big and small: in that very building seventy-five years before, scientist T. H. Huxley defended Darwin's revolutionary *Origin of the Species* against Bishop Samuel Wilberforce's claims that evolution was not real. In 1905, Polly Porter, an inspiration to Hodgkin, started working in the Oxford Museum with Henry Alexander Miers, who created Oxford's crystallography department.

Now, flash forward to 1936, a little over a year after Hodgkin's return to Oxford. This is when she took her first X-ray of insulin. This was a huge accomplishment. Insulin is incredibly important to every person's health. Without enough of it behaving as it should in the system, blood sugar levels rise to dangerous levels. This leads a person to develop diabetes, a disease that has serious effects on overall health. Proteins in general set the bar high for complicated molecules, and insulin is one of the trickiest proteins to understand. It would take Hodgkin and her team more than three decades to fully solve insulin's structure. However, photographing it was a big first step.

With her impressive work, Hodgkin had earned her doctorate, and she graduated from Cambridge, with Bernal as her advisor, in 1937. She wrote her thesis on the sterols research they did; Bernal's starting work with sterols had been the exciting work that had drawn her to transfer temporarily to Cambridge. That same year, she married Thomas Hodgkin, an expert in African and Middle East history and politics. As Dorothy Hodgkin followed in her family's footsteps, going into a research career, so her husband followed in the footsteps of his family of historians.

TRAILBLAZING THROUGH SOCIETY AS WELL AS SCIENCE

As a scientist who was also a wife and mother starting in the late 1930s, Hodgkin worked outside a very particular social norm for women. In 1930, according to the US Census, 24.3 percent of women worked outside the home; in 1940, 25.4 percent did. Most of these held clerical, factory, or domestic servant jobs. Some were teachers or nurses. Most worked for wages much less than men's pay. It was particularly difficult for married women to work. *Fortune* magazine polled its readers in 1936, asking, "Do you believe that married women should have a full-time job outside the home?" Only 15 percent of respondents offered unconditional approval. While 37 percent were okay with married women working in some cases, 48 percent disapproved wholeheartedly, in large part because they believed women should be home with their children.

Hodgkin and her husband had children soon after they married: Luke was born in 1938, Elizabeth in 1941, and Toby in 1946. In contrast to the norm reported by the US Census and polls such as *Fortune*'s, everyone who was important in Hodgkin's life supported her being a working mother. Her husband wanted her to continue to work, and she even sometimes worked under her maiden name. Her father and mother, having also been working parents, helped care for the kids. For a time, her family shared a home with her sister Joan and Joan's husband and five children, a situation that widened the network of support for these working parents and kids alike. And Hodgkin's employer, Somerville, offered paid maternity leave, a rarity in those days (and still not guaranteed by all employers today).

Hodgkin proved their belief in her correct, managing to be both a brilliant scientist and a loving mother. In his obituary for her, her friend and colleague Nobel Prize–winning chemist Max Perutz wrote that she could be motherly even while working; she was a multitasker, listening intently to her children and then solving equations with equal attention to detail.

A NEIGHBOR IN THE WORLD COMMUNITY

To the benefit of some people, Hodgkin went above and beyond in blending her roles as scientist and mother. In addition to her three biological children, she "adopted" many others, younger scientists with whom she worked in her laboratory. They were from twenty-one countries, including the United States, Australia, India, Canada, New Zealand, China, Denmark, Holland, Nigeria, the Soviet Union, and the United Kingdom, though most were not from her home country of England. Everyone knew her as nurturing and guiding, willing to open

Hodgkin had lots of interests outside of her work, including her family. Here she is with her oldest child, Luke.

her lab as quickly as she was to open her home. When Hodgkin was involved with a group, the group became like a family. She encouraged this communal feeling even in more public, formal ways. For instance, she sponsored the Society for Anglo-Chinese Understanding, which promoted friendship between British and Chinese people.

That she would conduct her life like this was not surprising. Hodgkin was raised to consider the world her neighborhood. With her parents traveling around Africa and the Middle East, she called nowhere and everywhere her home. She instilled the same message in her kids; all three studied and worked in various countries once they became adults.

As a member of the world community, Hodgkin didn't see the world as her playground—she saw it as a place where she lived and worked on a day-to-day basis, where her neighbors lived, and where she could do some good. That was certainly an attitude her mother had instilled in her. Tragedy helped to give her mother this perspective. All four of Hodgkin's uncles died in World War I, either directly in battle or as a result of their war injuries. Molly Crowfoot not only desperately missed her brothers but hated what she saw as the wastefulness of their deaths. They'd ended up dying so young, and the world seemed to be no better than it had been before the war—maybe it was even worse. As she mused on this, she thought she heard the voice of one of her brothers. He told her that making the world a better place was actually her job, and what their deaths had done was allow her to realize that.

At so many times in Hodgkin's life, she intersected with other luminaries making big changes in both their fields of work and world politics and affairs. She would become one of the most famous subjects of photographer Helen Muspratt, sitting for a portrait with Muspratt and her business partner, Lettice Ramsey, around 1937. One can only imagine that the three women connected over many aspects of their lives. Muspratt was, like Hodgkin and like Ramsey—who went to work after her husband died—also a major financial contributor to her household. Hodgkin had no problem collaborating with Communists, who were often vilified at that time, and Muspratt was a Communist, having become one after crossing into "enemy territory" to take pictures in the Soviet Union. Also like Hodgkin, Muspratt became involved in the peace movement, joining the Campaign for Nuclear Disarmament and Medical Aid for Vietnam.

After Hodgkin became chancellor of Bristol University in 1970, the Hodgkin Scholarship was established. It provided funding to students from developing countries. The Hodgkin House was built to house students visiting from overseas. (Both were named for Hodgkin's husband.)

As the president of the International Union of Crystallography, also in the 1970s, she allowed crystallographers from behind the Iron Curtain to participate in conferences. These were countries ruled by or with tight ties to the Soviet Union, in Eastern Europe, and considered enemies of Hodgkin's country and its allies. Her opinions about this did not sit well with the United States; there were restrictions on her US visa until 1990.

She gave the Azad Memorial Lecture, on "Wondering Scientists," in 1973 in India. The lecture series promotes understanding across nations. In 1987, she was awarded the Lenin Peace Prize for her commitment to peace. J. D. Bernal, her mentor and friend in matters both outside and inside the lab, had won the award in 1953.

PEACE AND JUSTICE WORK

Bernal himself did much for peace and justice, including helping to establish the J. D. Bernal Library, which opened in London in 1968 as a center for researching peaceful solutions to world issues. Hodgkin sponsored the library and was elected chair of the library board in 1971.

During the Vietnam War, Hodgkin's concern for peace leaped. She became vice president of the Medical Aid Committee for Vietnam in 1965 and president of it in 1971. Dr. Joan McMichael started the organization in 1965 after she visited Vietnam and realized how desperate the people were for medical attention. She asked Hodgkin to be the organization's first president, but Hodgkin declined because at that time she was busy helping elsewhere in the world: she was in Ghana frequently because her husband was setting up an African studies institute there. During Hodgkin's presidency of the Medical Aid Committee for Vietnam, the committee collected 6,567 pints of blood during a blood drive. Also as president, she visited North Vietnam in 1971 and 1974. This organization is still around today, now called Medical and Scientific Aid for Vietnam, Laos and Cambodia.

At about the same time, Hodgkin was one of the deputy chairmen of the International Commission of Enquiry into US Crimes in Indochina. It was established during the Fifth Stockholm Conference on Vietnam in 1970 to address violent crimes by the United States against Indochinese peoples. Hodgkin was honorary vice president for a project called the British Hospital for Vietnam, which sought to raise funds to build a hospital in North Vietnam.

In 1986, Hodgkin joined the Institute for International Peace Studies' International Advisory Board because, like the institute, she encouraged multidisciplinary research and teaching in issues of peace and justice. Scientists Against Nuclear Arms (SANA) requested she chair the opening session of its first conference to coordinate scientists halting nuclear arms use. For the International Scientists' Peace Congress, Ways Out of the Arms Race, in Hamburg in 1986, Hodgkin was a member of the advisory committee.

Though Hodgkin was not interested in flaunting her awards and honors, she was not opposed to making use of them. She was happy to claim her status as a Nobel Prize winner in order to speak on topics important to her. She gave a lecture at Science and Peace: The Nobel Laureates Answer in Paris in 1983.

THE MIRACLE MEDICINE

Ten years after Hodgkin started her investigation of insulin, she made a discovery that some might say would prove even more influential: she calculated penicillin's structure. She was thirty-five years old, and she held in her hands the answer to a large variety of health concerns. Yes, the answer was literally in her hands: she made a physical model of wires and corks, demonstrating the arrangement of atoms in penicillin. Often, scientists show their work with numbers, mathematical calculations incomprehensible to many people. However, sometimes, they break a discovery down.

Knowing the structure of penicillin was a game changer. Today, it's hard to imagine a world where penicillin is not commonplace. Because of penicillin, illnesses like strep throat and ear infections are now considered minor and easily treatable. But not that long ago, before Hodgkin's work, the smallest of infections could lead to fatal complications.

The History of Penicillin

The discovery of penicillin in 1928 was a serious feat that happened in a comical way. Scottish scientist Alexander Fleming was working on antiseptics for infections. His lab was a mess, Petri dishes stacked like so many dirty dishes in a sink. As he went to finally clean, he noticed that mold had started to grow on some of the dishes—and all around the mold, the staph bacteria that had been growing in the dishes had died. Fleming was witnessing penicillin in action.

Further exploration of the possibilities was slow going. Chemists were needed to really explore the possibilities, but there wasn't a dedicated team, and failures left researchers thinking penicillin might not be of practical use to medicine. Then, in 1940, scientists Howard Florey and Ernst Chain conducted an experiment that showed some promise—mice injected with both bacteria and penicillin lived weeks longer than those injected with just bacteria, which died within a day.

Hodgkin Joins the Effort to Understand Penicillin

War put the pressure on. Clinical trials in 1941 showed penicillin could be miraculous in humans. There were so many soldiers in World War II who needed this medicine, but it was still in its infancy and could not be mass-produced. Scientists needed to know the structure of penicillin to do that. Hodgkin was on the team of British and American scientists from universities and corporate laboratories in the United States and the United Kingdom working together to solve this.

As an X-ray crystallographer, Hodgkin needed penicillin crystals in order to determine penicillin's structure. The team of scientists developing this medicine did so collaboratively, with a spirit of international partnership. Hodgkin obtained some crystals also through community effort. Many people and organizations from different parts of the world helped her. In 1943, US pharmaceutical company Squibb isolated mold growing on a melon into a sodium salt called benzylpenicillin (later known as penicillin G). British chemist Robert Robinson, who would win the Nobel Prize in 1947, brought the crystals from the United States to Hodgkin. The British Royal Institute and the US military worked together to obtain and transport more needed crystals in 1944.

Hodgkin is known as pioneering the use of X-ray crystallography in complex organic substances like proteins. She was first in another way too: In the 1940s, she used IBM analog computers to help complete calculations. This was one of the first uses of a computer, and definitely the first time one was put to the task of solving a biochemical problem.

PRECIOUS CARGO

In the stories of crystallography, there are always fun little asides about people carrying crystals. The structures that crystallographers study are real, even if they're incredibly tiny, and so are the crystals they live in. A protein crystal, for example, may be 0.1 millimeters (0.004 inches), the size of the smallest grain of sand you can see. And within that speck are millions of molecules. Like a snow globe with a city built inside it, a crystal can hold a whole world too. When Hodgkin was working with Bernal on pepsin, other scientists were as well. John Philpot, a chemist and biochemist from Oxford, had made some pepsin crystals in Scandinavia. Glenn Millikan, a colleague of Bernal's and Philpot's, told Philpot that Bernal would do anything for some of those beautiful crystals. Philpot casually said he could just take a tube full of them, and Millikan carried them home to Oxford in his shirt pocket. In remembering this story later, Hodgkin suggested that the fact that they survived the journey in their mother liquor was "the important part, scientifically, of the story." To someone who isn't a scientist, this could be rather humorous. To photograph a complicated structure may seem like the true scientific advancement. Of course, to an advanced scientist such as Hodgkin, the intrigue is in the details. She knew that understanding how to handle crystals better would mean the world to future study.

B12 AND THE NOBEL PRIZE

Figuring out penicillin did not mean that Hodgkin took a vacation. The next challenge was always the goal—Hodgkin liked to work; she liked what she did. Her next puzzle was vitamin B12.

Humans don't naturally produce enough B12 for healthy living, so we must supplement with B12 from diet. If a person's diet is deficient or if a body can't absorb the vitamin, the effects can be fatal. If scientists knew its structure, they could, as with penicillin, understand how it reacts with the body and **synthesize** it.

After the vitamin was isolated in 1948, Hodgkin started looking at it. By 1961, she had a complete answer. While her mentor, Bernal, thought that she'd get the Nobel Prize for her work on penicillin, it seemed Hodgkin had to prove herself in a big way not once with penicillin but twice, with both penicillin and B12. And then she had to wait—she won the award three years after she calculated B12's structure.

Her friends seemed to mind the delay in international recognition of her work more than Hodgkin did. Max Perutz, who received the Nobel Prize for Chemistry two years before Hodgkin, said he was "embarrassed" to be recognized in such a way before she was, because she'd started having scientific success before he had. But Hodgkin did not think she deserved major international recognition by any particular time. Her acceptance speech for the Nobel Prize emphasized gratitude for the scientists who came before her and those who worked as her colleagues, "on whose hands and on whose brains I have relied." Her speech also expressed generosity, wishing for all her peers congratulating her to one day be standing at the place of honor. She told a story of attending a party in England the night before her trip to the Nobel ceremony in Sweden:

DOROTHY AND THE PUGWASH MOVEMENT

As invested as Dorothy Crowfoot Hodgkin was in science, she was passionate about social justice. Her work for peace took a great leap forward after the publication of the Russell-Einstein Manifesto in 1955.

Mathematician Albert Einstein also believed there was work to be done outside the classroom. He, philosopher Bertrand Russell, and many other leading intellectuals gathered in London in 1955 to express great concern about war and science's role in war. They feared that impressive advancements in technology, such as the creation of the atomic bomb, would also be humankind's downfall. They warned that people didn't even know the level of destruction possible because of the new technology. They called on scientists from all fields to join together to figure out what to do about this, working toward a peaceful end.

The Pugwash movement grew out of this manifesto. The group still brings together scientists and policy makers "to seek the elimination of all weapons of mass destruction, to reduce the risk of war especially in areas where weapons of mass destruction are present and may be used, and to discuss new scientific and technological developments that may bring more instability and heighten the risk of conflicts." Hodgkin was president of the group for more than a decade, until 1988.

During World War II, the British military asked her to join the war effort, but she was skeptical about that, and her boss agreed—she was, after all, working on penicillin at the time, and that seemed much more important!

Hodgkin, pictured here meeting fans of hers from the Swedish royal family, received the Nobel Prize in Chemistry in 1964.

> *My hosts advised me then, telling me how one should reply in Arabic to congratulations that one receives, congratulations on some very happy event: the birth of a son, perhaps or the marriage of a daughter. And one should reply: 'May this happen also to you.' And now even my imagination will hardly stretch so far that I can say this to every one in this great hall. But at least, I think, I might say to the members of the Swedish Academy of Science: 'In so far as it has not happened to you already, may this happen also to you!'*

ELSEWHERE IN X-RAY DIFFERENTIATION

This book celebrates Dorothy Crowfoot Hodgkin's life and work, but it would be wrong to ignore DNA as the most major discovery connected to X-ray differentiation. It was not one of Hodgkin's projects; though, because she was such an important scientist, she was invited to view the results privately before they were released to the public in 1953. Also, the story involves a scientist who was relatively excluded from history because she was a woman, as well as a scientist who worked as much for peace as he did for pure science, sometimes to the detriment of his science. Both shared commonalities with Hodgkin. This story also showcases X-ray differentiation as the multidisciplinary tool it is.

DNA, deoxyribonucleic acid, is the body's instruction manual. It's what makes us who we are. It's our structure. Everyone has unique DNA. We didn't know what DNA looked like, and therefore how it really worked, until 1953. Thanks to that discovery, we have made rapid advances in everything from gene therapy to forensics. We now know more about who we are and how genetic information is passed from parent to child.

Four scientists are linked directly to DNA's discovery: Rosalind Franklin, Maurice Wilkins, James Watson, and Francis Crick. Franklin studied chemistry at Cambridge in England and then X-ray crystallography in Paris. Her first job after her studies was to update the crystallography lab at King's College London in order to work on this strange thing called DNA. Wilkins was a Cambridge-trained physicist also working on DNA at King's College. He inadvertently got Watson, an American, interested in DNA when Watson heard Wilkins's speech at a zoology conference in 1951. Watson had studied zoology as well as genetics and viruses. He found work at the Cavendish Laboratory, where physicist Crick was working with Max Perutz, who was working with William Bragg (one of Hodgkin's teachers and mentors). Crick was supposed to be working on X-ray crystallography of hemoglobin, but Watson persuaded him to look to DNA instead.

Linus Pauling, an American chemist, was almost the fifth scientist in the race to discovery. He created the model-building method Watson and Crick ultimately used. Pauling's work had started people thinking of helixes, the form DNA has, but he ultimately proposed a three-stranded helix, and DNA is a double helix. Some people think he could have figured DNA out first, but he too would have needed Franklin's amazing, one-of-a-kind photographs, and he didn't stand a chance of getting them. He was outspoken in politics, as were some of his colleagues, including Hodgkin. Because of that, he was denied a passport by the US government for years. Ultimately, he was allowed to leave the country to accept the first of his two Nobel Prizes, in chemistry, in 1954, the year after DNA's discovery was announced. (He also won a Nobel for Peace in 1962.)

Rosalind Elsie Franklin was, like Hodgkin, a British chemist and crystallographer. Her role in the discovery of the structure of DNA changed the world forever.

Franklin had used X-ray diffraction and photographed DNA. Without Franklin's knowledge, Wilkins, along with Perutz, showed her work to Watson and Crick, and that was the key to the puzzle. Because of her photographs of two distinct forms of fibrous DNA, they knew that DNA was a double helix, and they knew its dimensions.

INSULIN, FINALLY

Hodgkin turned fifty-nine years old in 1969, and the world was in flux. There were wars, like the one in Vietnam, and fights for civil rights, growth in feminism, and the Stonewall riots. Hodgkin was about to take new steps, both in her career and in social justice. She had finally wrapped up what she had started more than thirty years ago. She'd finally calculated insulin's structure. In many ways, insulin was a defining substance for Hodgkin. Its role in her life started well before her first photographing it when she was in her twenties.

More Family Inspiration

When Hodgkin was fourteen, her mother connected her with their distant cousin Bobby, a biochemist. Later, he would be known widely as Sir Charles Robert Harington and would go on to hold such illustrious positions as director of the National Institute for Medical Research in Great Britain. His first news-making success was to isolate thyroxine, T4, a thyroid hormone used to treat hypothyroidism. It's also the thyroid hormone that, if it's being produced at low levels, causes hypothyroidism. Hypothyroidism is a condition in which the thyroid gland, which is located in the neck and helps to regulate growth and development, is underproducing. This can lead to feelings of fatigue and depression and, if untreated, serious concerns such as heart disease and pregnancy complications. His synthesizing of this thyroid hormone would have important medical implications. By understanding how thyroxine is structured, he could understand what it does and how, and he could replicate it in the lab. People naturally low in thyroxine could take his synthesized versions.

Hodgkin's mother asked her if she was inspired by their cousin's work discovery. Hodgkin said yes, and Molly wrote to Bobby for advice. He suggested D. S. Parsons's book *Fundamentals of Biochemistry*. In it, Hodgkin found a description of the isolation of insulin. She was fascinated by the hormone.

With the understanding of insulin's structure, scientists could understand how it helped lessen diabetic symptoms and modified it to increase its benefits. With Hodgkin's deciphering of insulin's structure, she again made a huge contribution to the medical community. She also made another professional leap forward. Vitamin B12 had been the largest molecule Hodgkin had been able to figure out. Now she'd had success on the other end of the spectrum. Insulin is one of the smallest protein molecules.

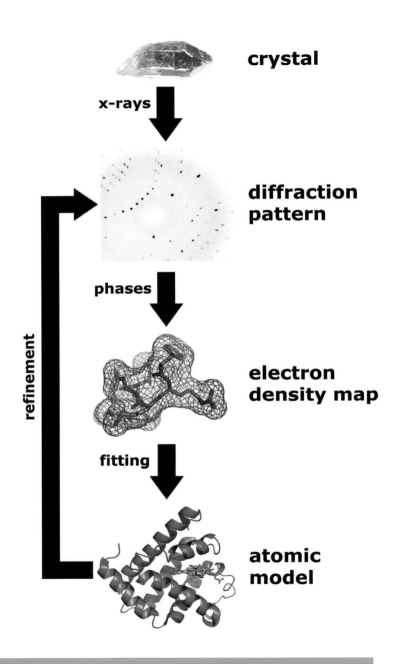

crystal

x-rays

diffraction pattern

phases

electron density map

fitting

atomic model

refinement

When you send X-rays through a crystal, a photograph of the inside of the crystal is created. Using math to "connect the dots," X-ray crystallographers can draw and then create 3-D models of molecules.

CHAPTER THREE

WHERE THERE'S A CRYSTAL, THERE'S A STRUCTURE; WHERE THERE'S A STRUCTURE, THERE'S UNDERSTANDING

I t can be so easy to skip wondering why an object is what it is and jump to immediately thinking about what it does. This is especially true today because we live at a time when we understand so much. Even if we ourselves don't understand something, we just expect that thing to do what it does because it has behaved that way a thousand times before. There was a time in the not-too-distant past when homes didn't have electricity; now, we flip a switch on the wall in even the most basic of structures, and the room is illuminated with light. We don't usually think about what is special about electricity that allows it to cast artificial light. We just think about how we need electricity in order to be able to see at night. But the only reason we can so casually incorporate something like electricity into our lives is because people before us figured out its properties. That's the role of X-ray crystallographers: to figure out what something is made of in order for us to understand it better. Specifically, they study anything that can be crystallized, and that includes many things, from biological building blocks to medicines and viruses and, yes, rocks and minerals.

WHY UNDERSTANDING WHY IS SO IMPORTANT

Because we know the structure of water, we can cook with it. The structure tells us at what temperature water boils (100 degrees Celsius and 212 degrees Fahrenheit). We know to press the graphite of pencil and not a diamond to paper because even though they're technically the same thing—carbon—they're completely different in structure. We know that muscles contract because they're made of two proteins, actin and myosin, and we know the structure of those proteins. So we know how they slide over each other repeatedly, and how two other proteins, tropomyosin and troponin, control actin and myosin. Again: because we know what makes tropomyosin and troponin tick, we know when they'll tick. Max Perutz talked about all of those whats and whys when he was trying to define why structural analysis is so important.

Why teeth are sometimes pink is another question that can be answered by studying a substance's composition. Hodgkin came across this interesting, and rare, phenomenon via the work of a family friend, Sir Archibald Garrod. He was retiring from Oxford not long before she entered the university, but before he left, she was able to secure a tour with him of the new biochemistry lab. In his research, Garrod had discovered a family with pink-tinted teeth. This was caused by the metabolism of porphyrins having gone astray. Porphyrins are chemicals that occur naturally in the body, but too many of them, and the body can start to look a little strange. For example, people suffering from some kinds of porphyria can have purplish urine (the word for these diseases comes from the Greek *porphyrus*, meaning "purple"). Understanding the structure of hematoporphyrin, a type of porphyrin, allowed Garrod to understand the reason for the strangely colored teeth. The story stuck with Hodgkin for the rest of her life. It was one of her early inspirations to learn the composition of something in order to understand what it does.

The father-and-son team of William and Lawrence Bragg figured out the structure of diamonds in 1913 and then, eleven years later, the structure of graphite. William Bragg came to be considered the father of X-ray crystallography, so his and his son's work really set the stage for Hodgkin's research and advancement of crystallography.

Diamonds are known to be incredibly hard. This can be seen when looking at a diamond's structure: carbon atoms are arranged in a three-dimensional tetrahedron, sturdy in all directions. It's no wonder a diamond isn't strong with a composition like that. Graphite is also made of carbon, but its atoms are arranged in two-dimensional hexagonal nets that can slide past one another. This makes graphite very soft, so soft that it leaves a mark when it's dragged across a surface. If we were going to make a pencil in a laboratory, we'd have to know how the atoms of graphite are arranged, or we could wind up making a diamond and leaving no mark at all. If we know the order of atoms in a substance, we know its material properties. Then we know what it does and what we can do with it.

We can thank crystallography and its practitioners, crystallographers, for allowing us to understand so much about the world around us.

WHAT IS CRYSTALLOGRAPHY?

Crystallography is a long word for the study of tiny things—some of the tiniest things known to us, atoms—and how they group together to form objects or substances. An atom is the smallest complete component of a substance, and everything is made up of atoms. Crystallographers, or scientists who study crystallography, also study molecules. Atoms that are joined together form molecules. So, everything is also made up of molecules. Atoms always arrange themselves the same way for each type of molecule. That's called a structure.

You may have seen all this represented with marbles connected by sticks. In those drawings or models, the marbles symbolize atoms and the sticks symbolize the bonds between atoms. Together, they form molecules. The marbles and sticks of a diamond look like a box, and the marbles and sticks of graphite are arranged like nets. If you had to guess how each substance would behave based on those two models, you might assume the one with the boxy structure would be stronger than the one that looks rather like something you could nap on. Again, we can see the big picture of a substance—how it will act in the world and how it will react with other things—once we know what it is by itself. How it is made, down to the smallest detail.

A SUMMARY OF HODGKIN'S SCIENCE

Hodgkin's science feels complicated in part because we don't experience it in our daily lives. It affects our daily lives, though. Because of it, we know what so many things in our world are, which means we can make use of those things and improve our lives. But we can't see or feel atoms, and we don't often interact with X-rays. Even if we did, we couldn't see those either.

Hodgkin was a pioneer in protein crystallography. Proteins are polymers, long chains of repeating units folded into three-dimensional shapes that are larger and more complicated than other biological molecules. The first video in a two-part Royal Institution video on understanding crystallography explains it well: Picture a long string of beads. That's the start of a protein molecule. Now let that string pile into your palm. It's a jumble, isn't it? That's what each protein molecule looks like. (Remember, this is just a helpful visual, not an exact representation of a protein molecule. A real protein molecule doesn't fold up in random ways as a string of beads does. It folds in a now predictable, known manner, but it looks about as complicated as that pile of beads.) If you were just figuring out what a protein molecule looked like, how could you begin to guess that complicated shape? You couldn't. You'd need to see it. But you couldn't do that because the molecule is much too small, even with a microscope.

In comes the use of X-rays. If you shoot a vial of protein with X-rays, you could see the molecules inside the protein, just as you would see the bones of your hand if you shot it with X-rays. Unfortunately, naturally, there are millions of these molecules floating around in one small tube of protein, turning this way and that. If you took an X-ray of a pond of fish, the image the X-ray produced would be confusing because at the time it was taken, the fish would be moving, and some would be facing one way and some the other. You wouldn't be able to tell from the X-ray image what a fish looked like because the rays would catch different parts of different fish. You would need to get the fish to tread water, all facing one way. That's what crystallization does to a substance. It forces the molecules to line up in one direction, equal spaces between them. This way, when you shoot X-rays at the molecules, the shadows they cast make an accurate picture of the tiny shapes.

UNDERSTANDING ATOMIC AND MOLECULAR STRUCTURE

Atoms and molecules and the way they arrange themselves in an object, which then makes the object, are very important to crystallography.

Understanding that is the whole point of that science. So, let's make sure the definitions of atoms and molecules and the way they work together in a structure are clear.

Consider this sentence: I am listening to music.

What are the pieces of the sentence? Words. Words put together make a sentence. Are words the smallest parts in a sentence, or can you cut the words into pieces? Yes, you can divide words into smaller parts: letters. Letters put together make words. Can you cut letters into anything smaller? Sure, you could write just a dot from an *i*, or you could cut the tail off a *g*, but that dot and that tail are not meaningful things on their own. So, no, letters are the smallest complete pieces of a word. And can you arrange the letters and words in any old way to form the same sentence? Is "I am listening to music" the same as "Ili amtostmusic icening"? Listening is always l-i-s-t-e-n-i-n-g, and music is always m-u-s-i-c, just like atoms always arrange a certain way for one molecule and another way for a different molecule. And the words, or molecules, must then also arrange themselves in a certain order.

Let's bring this back to crystallography. In this example, we could imagine each letter as an atom and each word as a molecule. Put together, they form a sentence. There can be no words without letters and no sentences without words.

We don't normally think of sentences in terms of atoms and molecules, but now that we understand the basic way those things work together, we can see how they work in things that scientists do study. Let's keep it simple by looking at something we use every day, usually more than once a day. Even if you haven't brushed your teeth, taken a shower, or held a glass under the kitchen faucet yet today, you've probably flushed the toilet—so, yes, you've probably used water today.

What is water? It's … just water. Right? Even something that seems so basic is made up of atoms and molecules. You may have heard water called H_2O. H stands for the atom hydrogen and O for the atom oxygen. Two hydrogen atoms bonded, or stuck together, with one oxygen atom makes one molecule of water. The molecules bond together at certain points: The oxygen atom of one molecule does not stick to the oxygen molecule of another. Instead, the oxygen of one always connects to the hydrogen of another. Now, go pour yourself 8×10^{24} molecules of water (that's about a glass full), and we'll get back to this book's hero: Dorothy Crowfoot Hodgkin.

You can't feel or see the atoms or molecules in your glass of water, so they must be extremely small. How does a scientist see which atoms and molecules make up a thing, and how those atoms and molecules stick together? How can you understand something whose parts you cannot see or feel? That was the challenge Hodgkin faced. Though she was far from the first chemist to look at the atomic and molecular structures of things, she helped make it easier to do so. Because she used a revolutionary technique, X-ray crystallography, she was able to make discoveries a lot sooner than scientists would have without the use of X-rays.

Chemists before her had to conduct lengthy experiments that took a lot of effort and probably were at least a little bit messy. Remember that penicillin was discovered basically because of a sink of dirty dishes. Even before those dishes found their way to the sink, they were dirty— Alexander Fleming had purposefully filled them with staph bacteria.

Emil Fischer was one such chemist who came before Hodgkin. He died only nine years after she was born, so when he was working, the world was a very different place from when Hodgkin was working. He might put a substance through reaction and degradation. This

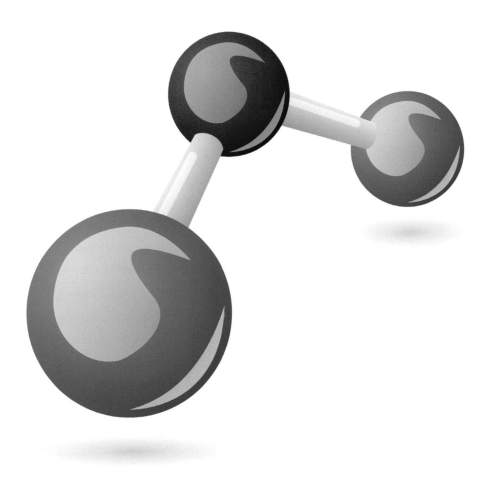

A water molecule's structure is two hydrogen atoms (shown here in blue) attached to one oxygen atom (red).

would help him hypothesize a molecular structure. Then, in order to check his work, he'd try to synthesize the substance. Fischer also used **oxidation** and **epimerization**. Picture a lab of bubbling liquids and sparking reactions. Hodgkin's work required no less brainpower or effort, but it required a vastly different kind of laboratory. Fischer had to physically manipulate substances. Because of their complicated and small structures, this was a lengthy process, and he could only expect to progress so far. There are limitations to all forms of experimentation. Scientists needed X-ray crystallography to take their research to the next level and learn about substances they could not have learned about before, at least not easily, such as proteins.

THE EARLIEST DAYS OF CRYSTALLOGRAPHY

Crystallography can be traced back to the late 1700s. While it has changed a lot in 250 years, one thing seems to have stayed the same: its ability to surprise even the most curious and open-minded of scientists. Hodgkin said her work often showed her a structure that completely surprised her. Crystallography itself started in 1781 with an unintentional fumble.

Crystallographers now study anything that can crystallize into an ordered set of molecules, which even includes things that don't seem very solid, like viruses, fibers, and gases. But the science started with a crystal more of the sort you might think of when you hear that word: a beautiful, jagged chunk of calcite. In 1781, Rene-Just Haüy, who would come to be considered the creator of crystallography, was looking at a friend's beautiful new piece of calcite when he dropped it. Picking through the pieces, he noticed that the mineral had shattered in a very unique way. The shards did not look like pieces of a broken cookie, each one ragged and different from the other. Instead, each piece had smooth sides that met at constant angles. He later broke the pieces further and found the pattern continued. No matter how small the piece, it always broke the same way—he couldn't make it break along different lines or crumble it. This was the start of a theory of crystal structure.

Through the 1800s, scientists like Ludwig Seeber, Gabriel Delafosse, August Bravais, Leonhard Sohncke, Arthur Schoenflies, and Evgraf Fedorov continued the experimentation. Then, in April 1912, Max von Laue did something for which he'd win the Nobel Prize: he created X-ray crystallography, which Dorothy Hodgkin would use to change the world.

MODERN CRYSTALLOGRAPHY
The Definition and Function of X-Rays

Let's begin by understanding what X-rays are. X-rays were not known until 1895, when Wilhelm Röntgen discovered them. (He too would win a Nobel Prize, for his work with X-rays.) Röntgen was studying a different kind of ray of light, called a cathode. He noticed that a screen coated in a special substance glowed when he aimed the cathode rays through the X-ray tube, but he knew that the rays could not be striking the screen and causing the glow; they couldn't travel that far. That meant there had to be other rays of light, which he hadn't known existed, also present and traveling farther than the cathode rays. Röntgen held his hand up between the X-ray tube and the screen and saw his bones projected on the screen!

X-rays are rays of light. X-rays have a short wavelength, which allows them to pass through objects. This is important because this allows us to see inside objects. Think about the use of X-rays that most of us know: photos taken of the human body for medical reasons.

Think about how you cast a shadow when visible light, from the sun or a flashlight, hits you. Bones, which are denser than other parts of the body, cast shadows when X-rays hit them. In a medical X-ray, doctors pay attention to that. Crystallographers pay attention to what else happens: that some of the light scatters.

THE ELECTROMAGNETIC SPECTRUM

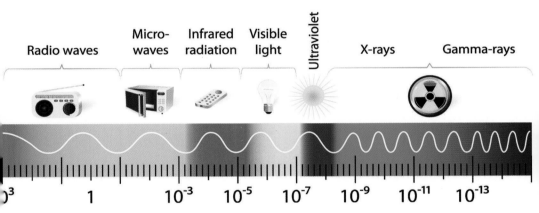

The electromagnetic spectrum shows different kinds of light waves and where X-rays fit in that series.

The Unique Way X-Rays Travel

When an X-ray strikes an atom, something interesting happens. Most of the light—more than 99 percent of it—passes through the atom. The small bit of remaining light scatters, shooting out from the atom in different directions. A very small particle of matter that has a negative electric charge, called an electron, travels around an atom.

THE X-RAY ANALYSIS OF COMPLICATED MOLECULES, NOBEL LECTURE, DECEMBER 11, 1964

Each Nobel Laureate, or recipient of a Nobel Prize, gives a Nobel Lecture prior to the Nobel Prize Award Ceremony. This excerpt is from Hodgkin's presentation:

" *Our early attempts at structure analysis now seem to be very primitive. The crystal structures of cholesteryl chloride and bromide proved not sufficiently isomorphous to solve by direct-phase determination. We moved over to cholesteryl iodide, where the heavier atom was both easier to place in the crystal from the Patterson synthesis and contributed more to the scattering. Harry Carlisle showed it was possible to place the atoms in three dimensions by calculating sections and lines in the three-dimensional electron-density distribution with phases derived at first from the iodine contributions alone; it took him months to make calculations on Beevers-Lipson strips which now would take fewer hours. The atomic arrangement found completely confirmed the sterol formula as revised by*

Rosenheim and King and Wieland and Dane, following Bernal's first X-ray measurements. We sought for a compound of more unknown structure.

We were encouraged to try our operations on penicillin by Chain and Abraham before ever the antibiotic itself was crystallized; I grew crystals for X-ray analysis from 3 mg of the sodium salt flown over during the war from the Squibb Research Institute to Sir Henry Dale; the crystals were grown under the watchful eyes of Kathleen Lonsdale, who brought them to me from London. Later, we also grew crystals of potassium and rubidium benzyl-penicillin, hoping again for an isomorphous series. But first the sodium salt was not isomorphous with the other two, then the potassium and rubidium ions were in such positions in the structure that they did not contribute to many of the reflections. ″

The X-ray's interaction with the electron causes a small amount—less than 1 percent—of its light to diffract, shoot out from, or scatter.

- *Think of an atom as a marble.*
- *Think of an X-ray as an arrow.*
- *The arrow shoots toward the marble.*
- *Most of the arrow continues on through the marble; pieces of it break off and scatter in different directions from the marble.*

Laue's Groundbreaking Experiments

Even after Röntgen's discovery, X-rays were mysterious for many years. Beyond not knowing what use they could have, scientists weren't even sure what they were. Laue's experimentation proved that X-rays are a form of electromagnetic radiation. Radio waves, visible light, and infrared light are other forms of electromagnetic radiation.

Once he knew what X-rays were, Laue could start to imagine what they could do. That sounds like Hodgkin's work too. She knew that we need to know the structure of things like penicillin and B12—in other words, what those things are—before we can know what they do and how we can use them.

Knowing that X-rays are electromagnetic, Laue wanted to see how they would react when they came in contact with an object, specifically with each of the object's atoms. Remember that Haüy's fortunate accident showed how smoothly crystals break. So it was assumed that the atoms within them were lined up in even, regular intervals. Laue further guessed that X-rays could fit through the spaces between atoms in crystals. He felt he could learn something by seeing how

William Bragg's ionization spectrometer was the prototype of all modern X-ray diffractometers, such as this one.

X-rays moved through crystals. He shot an X-ray through a crystal, with a photographic plate on the other side, to capture an image of what happened. Even after looking at the images, he wasn't sure what he was learning.

That was all right. Just trying—not necessarily understanding or succeeding—is an important part of science. The scientists who continued Laue's work agreed. William Bragg, the father in the father-son team who took X-ray crystallography to the next level, admired Laue for creating a new science.

Fourier Transform

Just as Röntgen lived before his X-ray discovery could be used to its full extent with crystallography, so Jean-Baptiste Joseph Fourier (1768–1830) lived before his mathematical discovery could become the mathematical underpinning of crystallography. So he did not figure out this equation with structural biology in mind, but it's turned out to be quite useful for that. If you use the Inverse Fourier Transform to measure the scattering, you can work out mathematically the shape of the molecule. It's basically a description in numbers of what a substance's structure looks like. Lord Kelvin, an Irish mathematical physicist, thought it was a stunning analysis for the modern world, and he'd be quite right that it would continue to hold up with each passing day.

Bragg's Law

When he got word of Laue's work, William Bragg was already a physicist working on X-rays. He also had written the book for children on X-rays, *Concerning the Nature of Things,* that first inspired Hodgkin. His son Lawrence was a university student. Together, they figured out how to

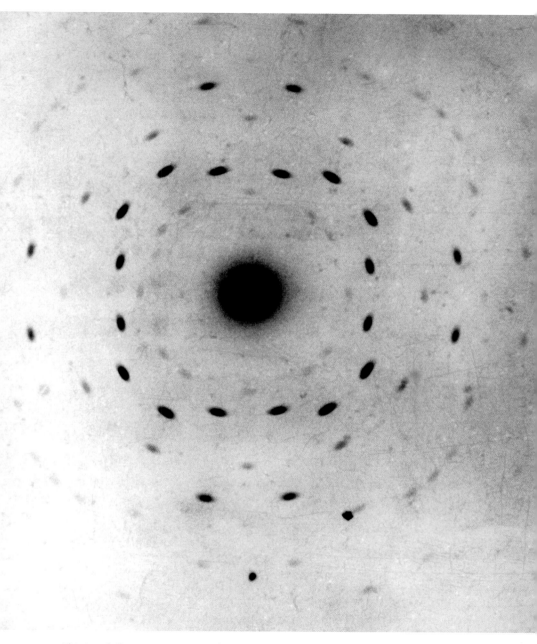

This is a diffraction pattern made on paper by X-rays shot through a crystallized substance.

make sense of the images Laue first created, and they expanded on his work.

Remember—we're picturing atoms as marbles. In crystals, these marbles appear in evenly spaced rows, layered upon each other in planes. Picture a box packed with marbles, the marbles sitting on top of, underneath, and next to each other in an orderly fashion. It's not a jumbled mess; it's a nicely packed cube of marbles. Atoms are teeny, so in a crystal, there are millions of planes of atoms.

Young Lawrence, a student, realized the X-rays were passing not in the spaces between the atoms but reflecting off the planes of atoms. Using trigonometry, he determined what has become known as Bragg's law. In math and science, a law describes an observed phenomenon; it is a statement based on repeated experimentation. Bragg's law states in which direction there will be scattering, depending on the angle an X-ray is sent into a crystal, and the spacing is an indication of the structure of atoms within a crystal.

We have been thinking of rays of light as arrows. For just a moment, so you get the idea of the movement of light, think of it as a ball, as one of those really bouncy little rubber superballs. If light were a superball and you threw it at the ground, it would bounce back up. Remember that if you could throw an X-ray like a superball, most of it would continue on that path and pass through the floor. But little bits of it would break off and fly in different directions. Now we have to start thinking three-dimensionally. Think about that box of marbles again. In your imagination, remove the box, but keep the marbles together in that nicely packed cube. That's your crystal with its neat atomic structure. If you look at it from one direction, it appears like a sheet, not a box, and you can picture an X-ray (arrow) hitting it from one side, most of the light traveling through the marbles from left to right but some of it scattering off to the same angle in a different direction. But this cube is not a sheet; it is a cube. There are other planes, or layers, of atoms in it. Slowly move around the cube. You can see rows of marbles along the horizontal, the vertical, and the diagonals.

The spots in a **diffraction pattern** are all the various reflections that are allowed by Bragg's law. Some dots are darker than other dots, and that indicates that the X-ray that left that dot on the paper hit a spot with a lot of electrons. All of this tells a scientist where the atoms inside the crystal are.

By December 1912, Lawrence Bragg, only twenty-two years old, was the first person to solve the atomic structure within a crystal. He wrote to his dad, William, that it had all been right in front of Laue. Laue could have gotten it had he been approaching the puzzle from this angle. Lawrence thought it was a lot of fun that he had figured it out.

William Bragg developed the X-ray spectrometer to get a better handle on this. A narrowly focused X-ray could be shot at a crystal suspended in the machine. By adjusting the angle of the X-ray, Bragg worked his way around the crystal. He measured not only the angle the light shot from the crystal but the intensity with which it shot. Different angles produced different intensities. Using his son's calculations, he realized he was seeing the arrangement of atoms. Try this yourself by playing with the angles of X-rays (the lines) and the spacing of atoms (the blue dots) in this interactive image: http://www-outreach.phy.cam. ac.uk/camphy/xraydiffraction/xraydiffraction_exp.htm.

Maybe at this point we should imagine Dorothy Hodgkin as her friend and colleague Max Perutz described her in his obituary of her. He said that often a dreamy look would cross her face during meetings, as all the scientists around the table discussed and argued about the problem at hand and its possible solutions. And then without warning she'd speak, some spot-on observation that no one else had seen. She might have been considered a know-it-all except that she presented so warmly, her corrections of others' work always followed by a little laugh to soften her words.

Hodgkin always followed the thrill of the chase, the excitement of following the math and the science along a twisting journey to, ultimately, a rewarding conclusion, completely logical in its existence but completely surprising.

INSPIRING CONTEMPORARIES

Hodgkin came from a line of scientists who thrilled to the chase—after all, that's what scientists do! But it is particularly exciting to learn of women's professional advances because for too long we haven't heard much about any scientific work by women.

Polly Porter

Mary "Polly" Porter worked during Hodgkin's time. She had been assistant to Henry Alexander Miers, the man who transformed Oxford University's mineralogy department into a crystallography lab in the late 1800s. Porter had a surprisingly long effect on X-ray crystallography and became an inspiration to Hodgkin.

Porter's influence was surprising in large part because she left school before she was fifteen. Her parents didn't think she needed an education, but they couldn't stop her from learning on her own. She did such a good job with her self-designed study that she ended up unintentionally impressing Miers. He took notice of her regular visits to the Oxford Museum's collection of antique Italian marbles and asked if she could translate the catalog from Italian. She could.

Despite such a well-known academic being in their daughter's corner, Porter's parents refused to let her attend Oxford. That attitude continued to have little actual effect on her life. She continued to be offered, and to happily take, research opportunities not only in England but also in the United States and Germany, and eventually she found herself working in X-ray crystallography. Miers simply asked her if she would like to try growing some crystals. Encouragement is an important component to someone's education being a success. Porter published in respected journals and coedited the three-volume *Barker Index of Crystals*.

Kathleen Lonsdale

Also one of Hodgkin's contemporaries, Kathleen Lonsdale became well known in their shared field of crystallography. "There is a sense in which she appeared to own the whole of crystallography in her time," Hodgkin once said of her. Like Hodgkin, Lonsdale worked under William Bragg and upheld his legacy. Hodgkin looked up to her, not only for her success but also for the fact that Lonsdale continued to work while raising three children. In turn, Lonsdale admired Hodgkin's ability and played a role in Hodgkin's penicillin research by growing, and even transporting, some crystals Hodgkin used.

Given the era in which she lived, Lonsdale was lucky when it came to her success. With a scholarship, she attended a girls' high school, but she had to take some of her classes at the boys' school—physics, chemistry, and math simply weren't offered at her school. She was the only one of the ten children in her family who went to high school. Back then, education wasn't as common as it is now. A lot of people we would consider of school age today were, as late as the mid-1900s, already working full-time jobs. Her siblings left school to work in order to support their family.

Hodgkin greatly admired her colleague in crystallography, Kathleen Yardley Lonsdale, not only for her research but for her ability to keep working while raising a family.

Dorothy Hodgkin: Biochemist and Discoverer of Protein Crystallography

In later life, physicist Lonsdale blazed many trails. For instance, she was one of the first women to be elected to the Royal Society and was the first female professor to be given a permanent position at University College London. She was the first to apply the Fourier mathematical methods to analyze X-ray patterns to atomic structure. In another exciting project, Lonsdale ended a sixty-year-old argument about the benzene ring, the six carbon atoms of benzene, arranged in a circle: yes, it was flat.

Margery Fry was a major influence on Hodgkin—in her schoolwork and her interest in social advocacy.

OBSTACLE COURSES AND SUPPORT SYSTEMS

Crystallography had an uphill battle to widespread public acknowledgment. X-ray crystallography is less visible to most people than the work of people such as Marie Curie and Albert Einstein. (Although isn't that rather perfect, that a technique used to see the unseeable is itself unseen?)

Hodgkin was herself low-key, even though she was one of the most well-known crystallographers. She chose projects not for the possibility of fame or money. She was fascinated in the science and if a structure would be interesting to investigate. She never wrote a book, led a glitzy laboratory, or listed any of her awards and honors as part of her name.

CRITICISMS OF CRYSTALLOGRAPHY

Early crystallographers faced some critics. Sometimes, the biggest arguments came from people who weren't experts in science. Johann Wolfgang von Goethe—who wrote the classic *Faust*, among many other pieces—was a renowned literary figure even when he was alive, in the late 1700s and early 1800s. For a while, he fancied himself a scientific thinker and criticized crystallography as having "no practical influence in a living context; for its most precious products, crystalline gems, first have to be cut and polished before we can use them to adorn our womenfolk." Wouldn't he have been surprised to have met Hodgkin, who did not wear her gems but studied them?

As early as 1895, the year X-rays were discovered, *Geological* magazine was supporting crystallography. Goethe knew crystallography before its geometrical principles had been fully established and when the technique was still used in mineralogy alone. By the turn of that century, chemistry, petrology, and geology made use of crystallography. Later, crystallography occasionally heard from detractors. Henry Armstrong, a chemist, responded to William Bragg in *Nature* in 1927, saying that X-ray physics offered false hope.

A MIXED RESPONSE TOWARD WOMEN IN THE FIELD

Men Supporting Women

Hodgkin repeatedly stated that being a woman did not cause her problems at work. Helen Megaw, who studied at Cambridge with Dorothy, agreed with that statement. There is a general consensus that X-ray crystallography was "largely hospitable" to scientists who were women.

Many men support women in the sciences (and in life) by being allies, both by speaking up for women and by getting out of their way so they can make their own choices and take leadership. Mathematical crystallographer Maureen Julian has done several studies of her field. In one, she listed all the scientists directly "related" through work to

Braggs; as of 1990, he'd had a direct effect on fifty crystallographers who were women.

Peter Lyttle, a program coordinator for the United States Geological Survey (USGS), shared a story about one of the women in Hodgkin's extended "family" of mentors, Florence Bascom, the first woman the USGS ever hired. In the 1980s, Lyttle was mapping some land, which required him to do physical work outside. One day, a man stopped his car and engaged Lyttle in conversation. Why was he messing with Bascom's work, the man demanded to know. Bascom had worked at a turning point in geology; she prepared folios, geologic maps of areas for the USGS, and also worked at the microscopic level of the study of rocks. Lyttle quickly explained he was not undoing or redoing her work, just updating it. Lyttle said he knew he "was standing on the shoulders of a giant."

An Expectation of Female Colleagues

As for women helping women in the field, there has been a bit of indifference. This is not because women don't want others to succeed; because the science has been so relatively egalitarian for so long, it may not seem as crucial that women support each other. Or perhaps the women drawn to the field are more focused on crystallography's success than the success of individuals.

Susan Lea, a microbiologist who studied structural biology for her PhD, said that she didn't even think about putting particular effort into securing a female scientist role model because they were all around her. Judith Howard, one of Hodgkin's students at Oxford, chose crystallography in part because there seemed to be plenty of women doing what she wanted to do, something Howard had never known before—even at her all-girls' school, the chemistry teacher was male. It drove Hodgkin nuts that the media called only on her whenever they needed to talk to a "female scientist": how "boring" to speak to just one person when there were plenty of options. However, nothing in life, including this, is clear-cut.

Men Not Supporting Women

More than once have men been given credit or taken credit for work they did not do or did not complete first. The *New York Times* misappropriated the vitamin B12's structure solution to Alexander Todd at the University of Cambridge, and the Chemical Society at the University of Exeter asked Todd to speak first at the organization's 1955 meeting. Hodgkin, whose Oxford team was the first to solve B12's structure, thankfully was present and publicly explained the true order of credit due.

Think of one of the biggest controversies in science: who figured out DNA's structure first. Francis Crick and James Watson are widely understood to be the discoverers. Rosalind Franklin is hardly known at all, but when she is mentioned, she is discussed as the X-ray crystallographer who played a supporting role in their work. That may not be the complete story. After earning her doctorate in chemistry at Cambridge University, Franklin spent three years learning X-ray diffraction techniques at a lab in Paris. She then returned to England to be a research associate in a lab. She led one of two groups researching DNA. Maurice Wilkins was the leader of the other group. He was out of the office when Franklin started working in the lab, and when he returned, he assumed she was an assistant, not his equal. The university did consider women of lesser importance than men, even in small matters. The university dining rooms as well as the after-hours breaks at the pubs were men only. Wilkins's incorrect perspective may have cost Franklin more than some social meals and happy hours; she came very close to solving the DNA structure, but Crick and Watson's work was printed before hers in part because she wasn't seen as deserving fair treatment.

Women Being the Odd Ones Out

Hodgkin's first chemistry class in school was made up of nearly all boys—except for her and one other girl, Norah Pusey. Pusey did better than Hodgkin in chemistry, yet she left school for a college that taught her how to care for the home, essentially, making her a housewife, which was common at the time. She wrote to Hodgkin that she hated her new school and was envious of Hodgkin sticking with chemistry, which they both loved. Still, Pusey had made the decision to leave. Ultimately, she just didn't think she could have made a living as a scientist. Better to do the "woman's work" that she was expected to do. In the face of society telling her what opportunities she should expect and that she wasn't capable at anything else, Pusey couldn't believe what her high grades were actually telling her.

She was far from the only woman who felt this way. Molly Crowfoot expressed concern to the teacher of two of her other daughters that Dorothy wouldn't get into college. The woman assured Molly that Dorothy would because Dorothy wanted to study science and so few girls did so. The university would find her a novelty.

This perception continues today. One science historian said that science businesses continue to want more women in their ranks because there simply aren't enough there already. The International Union of Crystallography's online list of scientists is 90 percent male. Its Ewald Prize has had one female recipient since 1987.

A STABLE AND VAST NETWORK: INSPIRATIONS AND CONTEMPORARIES

In 1971, at a meeting of biomedical researchers, women were invited to an evening cocktail hour to discuss the difficulties they faced as women in the male-dominated sciences. These challenges included job discrimination, not being selected for a job because of gender; receiving lower pay than men doing similar work; and being ostracized or ignored at work because their male colleagues didn't think they belonged there. Twenty-seven women showed up to the cocktail hour. The conversation they had did not end that night. They kept the conversation going and founded the Association for Women in Science. This organization still works to make sure women and men are treated equally while working in science, math, and technology.

Hodgkin didn't have such an organization for most of her life and career, but she was part of an informal network of women scientists. She didn't care for the term "role model," but there were several women who inspired her. Some she worked alongside; some she never knew, but together they form a powerhouse of related visionaries. They all played a role—with or without her knowledge, directly or indirectly—in her success.

Margery Fry (1874–1958)

Dorothy Hodgkin's and Margery Fry's circles overlapped before they met. Fry's sister ran the school two of Hodgkin's sisters attended. Soon after, Hodgkin met Fry at Somerville College, a women's school that was part of Oxford University. Hodgkin was a student, and Fry was the principal. They would become friends and remain inspirations for each other until Fry's death.

Throughout her life, Fry demonstrated her impressive intelligence and leadership skills. She studied math at Somerville and was the school's librarian, in addition to being its principal. For her service, today one of the campus buildings is known as Margery Fry House. She held many top roles outside of academia as well. She served on the board of governors of the BBC. In 1921, she was appointed a magistrate; she was one of the first female magistrates. As a layperson, meaning in this case a citizen without legal qualifications, she helped make decisions in court cases.

In this role, she focused on her lifetime passion: prison reform and the abolishment of the death penalty. Fry was born into a Quaker family and found her life's purpose by following that faith-based community's tenets of pacifism and social justice. By the time she became a magistrate, she'd already been secretary of a penal-reform organization. After her appointment, she was named education advisor to a women's prison in London. Governments eventually took notice of her international lobbying efforts. For example, in 1963, New Zealand was the first country to fund a crime victims compensation program. Fry felt that such victims were owed something just as sufferers of accidents on the road or at work were.

Though Hodgkin was dedicated to her work in the lab, she was just as much a member of the world. Her admiration of Fry is part of what encouraged her own peace and social reform work.

They were also important to each other as part of the same network of intellectuals and revolutionaries who also happened to be women. For example, when William Bragg invited Hodgkin to photograph insulin crystals at the Royal Institution in London, she stayed with Fry. Also staying there was young Pamela Nicolson, daughter of mathematician Dorothy Wrinch, who was also Fry's contemporary.

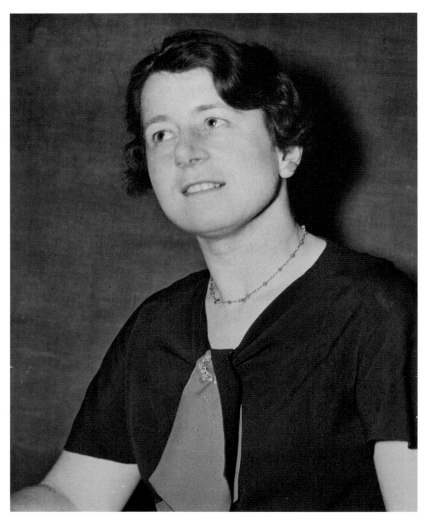

At a time when women weren't supposed to go to college and have careers, Dorothy Maud Wrinch was ahead of the curve, standing up for her research even when it was criticized.

Dorothy Wrinch (1894–1976)

Dorothy Wrinch's and Dorothy Hodgkin's life stories share similarities. For instance, Dorothy Wrinch was a British citizen born abroad; her father was an engineer stationed in Argentina. She too studied in

England and was the only woman in her math class. She became the first woman to lecture in math at Oxford University. Wrinch also wrote and published several papers and books—192 in all.

She earned her master's degree in mathematics in 1920 and began studying for her PhD in the same field, but by the 1930s, she'd switched to molecular biology and started addressing biological problems with math.

Her work focused on proteins, as Hodgkin's did, and she put forth a new model of proteins' structure. Her model was considered controversial because she stepped into a contentious issue with an unpopular view, and people took notice: in 1937 she went on a lecture tour in the United States, and the *New York Times* covered her talk at the American Philosophical Society in 1940.

Linus Pauling disagreed loudly with Wrinch's premise. This led to a public argument between the two in the *Journal of the American Chemical Society*. Some British X-ray crystallographers also attacked Wrinch, saying that despite her claims, X-ray data did not support her model. Wrinch eventually proved the cyclol bond that had caused so much hostility among her colleagues by using X-rays and the Fourier equation. She went on to spend more than twenty years focused on the importance of proteins in biology.

Max Perutz (1914–2002)

A longtime collaborator and friend of Hodgkin, Max Perutz was also one of her biggest champions, often speaking of her intelligence and skill, her humanity, and her worthiness of accolades. This was high praise, since Perutz himself was considered both influential in science and likable in life.

Born in Austria, Perutz started his studies at Vienna University, but he soon transferred to Cambridge, where he worked with Bernal, as Hodgkin did. Not long after, Hitler invaded Austria, and Perutz's parents and siblings fled, becoming refugees, depending on Perutz for help resettling in other countries. (Though Catholic in religious belief, they were Jewish in ancestry.) Perutz was lucky to have already been living in Great Britain at this time. When Germany annexed Austria in 1938, England considered any Austrian citizens living within its borders "enemy aliens." Perutz was questioned and considered to be not a threat. He was lucky for a second time. Then Germany invaded Norway and the Netherlands. This time, Perutz faced great, unreasonable consequences. He was one of the seven thousand Austrian and German nationals who were sent from Britain to internment camps in Canada. Internment camps are basically prisons for people whose "crime" is that they are considered enemies of the country they live in and people who express political beliefs different from those in charge (political prisoners).

Fortunately, Perutz's luck reappeared just in time: both Caltech and MIT, universities in the United States, offered him fellowships, funded by the Rockefeller Foundation, and his British colleagues protested so loudly that he was allowed to return to England. It was England's turn to be lucky: the country was smart to allow back in one of its most promising minds. Using X-ray crystallography, Perutz determined the structure of hemoglobin, the protein molecule in blood that carries oxygen to the body's tissues and carbon dioxide back to the lungs. He also studied the texture and flow of glaciers, via their crystals, which also allowed him to pursue two of his other loves, mountain climbing and skiing. Like Hodgkin, he looked beyond the laboratory and had a sense of humor. He published many essays, including a collection with the attention-grabbing title *I Wish I'd Made You Angry Earlier: Essays on Science, Scientists and Humanity.*

Max Perutz was a good friend of Hodgkin's, and he won the Nobel Prize in Chemistry just two years before she did.

Helen Megaw (1907–2002)

It's not every day that a person receives an award for work and definitely not every day that one gets an honor as unique as scientist Helen Megaw did: she was awarded an island. Her first research project as an X-ray crystallographer was on the structure of ice, and in acknowledgment, there's now an island in the Antarctic named after her, Megaw Island (at 66°55'S, 67°36'W).

She studied with J. D. Bernal at Cambridge at the same time Hodgkin did. In fact, she played a key role in Hodgkin's pepsin work with Bernal. They were struggling with making their pepsin crystals usable. Unfortunately, sometimes in order to study something, you end up harming or even destroying it. Think of the measures museums go to control light, temperature, and moisture levels around an artifact or piece of artwork, as well as how many hands, with and without gloves, touch it. In order to study and admire the piece, we put it at risk of damage by those kinds of forces. X-rays are so powerful that they also can do damage to the crystals scientists wielding the X-ray tube are trying to study. Megaw had developed a technique of freezing a crystal inside a Lindemann glass tube of heavy water. This tube acted as a protective barrier to help preserve the crystal during study. Hodgkin and Bernal used Megaw's method, and the next photograph they took was hugely successful.

Both Megaw and Hodgkin seemed to have natural talent with crystal structures. One of Megaw's post-doctoral assistants wrote in her obituary that Megaw could turn a structure around in her mind, see all its angles before actually drawing it, and then draw it correctly. Those are mental gymnastics usually left to computers these days.

Megaw had another interesting connection to Hodgkin. She suggested a collaboration of crystallographers, artists, and manufacturers to pattern fabrics, plates, and wallpaper, among other items, with designs. All of the designs would be inspired by atomic structures discovered by crystallographers. These were displayed at the Festival of Britain, a celebration of Great Britain, in 1951. Hodgkin's mother and sister Elisabeth, textile experts, likely would have found that very exciting indeed.

Rosalind Franklin (1920–1958)

Though her life was tragically short, ended by ovarian cancer, Rosalind Franklin, a contemporary of Hodgkin's, made one of the biggest impacts on life as we know it—because she helped figure life out. Her data, calculated from her X-ray diffraction images, was the data Francis Crick and James Watson used to understand the double helix of DNA, the carrier of our genetic makeup.

After a lot of persuading, her father allowed her to study not to be a social worker, as he wanted her to be, but to be a scientist as she wanted to be, and as her high grades in physics and chemistry supported. She earned her doctorate in physical chemistry from Cambridge in 1945. J. D. Bernal was a big admirer of her X-ray image of DNA. If she hadn't died so early in her career, and less than two years after learning she was sick, she likely would have changed the world even more. When she died, she was working on the tobacco mosaic virus, a disease of over 350 different plant species, and the polio virus.

With the establishment of the Rosalind Franklin Society, there is hope that more women will do such important work but with more acknowledgment by peers and public alike. The organization encourages and motivates scientists who are women.

Isabella Karle (1921–)

Another contemporary of Hodgkin's era, Isabella Karle had started working at the young age of twelve—in a cigar factory, no less, filling boxes with hand-rolled cigars. But in her spare time, she taught herself to read, in both English and Polish—she was an immigrant to the United States. She also taught herself math. Because of her self-education, she was able to improve her career options vastly.

Before Karle even started school, she was doing the accounting on some of her parents' restaurant bills. Impressed with her work, her mom taught her to read and write in Polish. So, even though Karle didn't know English when she started school at six years old, she was able to pick her studies up quickly. She skipped a total of three grades before high school. There, she was to take chemistry, physics, or biology, and she picked chemistry, which had a female teacher. That teacher was not the last to encourage Karle in her science studies. Her college chemistry teacher—a man—noticed her excellent work and told her matter-of-factly that she was going to graduate school. By the time she was twenty-three years old, after many classes in which she was the only woman, she had earned her PhD.

She married one of her fellow chemistry students, and together they made some revolutionary advances in structure analysis. Jerome Karle would later win a Nobel Prize in Chemistry for developing mathematical formulas for understanding crystals. He usually approached problems through their calculations, and his wife was the experimenter. She taught herself X-ray crystallography to try to put his numbers into action. Karle's electron diffraction apparatus allowed for analysis of even mismatched X-ray wavelengths and intervals between atoms. Hodgkin's work helped speed the analysis process, and today's computers and synchrotrons are doing so again; in between these two advancements,

Karle's work created a midpoint leap. Annual published analyses of structures grew from 150 to over 10,000 with her technique. Though the Karles did not share the Nobel Prize, Isabella would eventually receive recognition in her own right. She was "surprised and pleased that the women engineers were the ones who gave me my first award," the Women in Science and Engineering's Lifetime Achievement Award.

She and her husband both went on to the **Manhattan Project**, a US-government–funded research project that created the atomic bomb. Karle did not work directly on the bomb; however, it was still a dangerous place to work. One time when Karle was walking past the Coca-Cola soda fountain, her radiation meter blared. The soda delivery man had unknowingly used an infected hose to fill the machine.

Looking back on her career, which included a long time with the Naval Research Laboratory, she fondly recalled that she'd done what she loved, faced no real catastrophe, and had been recognized for her work.

Barbara Rogers-Low

Barbara Rogers-Low was Hodgkin's colleague during her work on the structure of penicillin. Together, they measured the bond distances between atoms in the penicillin molecule with impressive accuracy. To do this, they used X-rays and the Fourier method. This was considered huge in part because it was the first time X-ray data was solely used to map a molecule's structure; the fact that it happened with a molecule as complex as penicillin seems almost over-the-top impressive.

J. D. Bernal (1901–1971)

In this abbreviated list of Hodgkin's peers, John Desmond Bernal is singled out because he was so essential in Hodgkin's life. Perhaps he worked well with Hodgkin, first a student of his and then a colleague, romantic partner, and friend, in part because he grew up with a strong mother. Though Bernal was Irish, his mom was American and was a member of the one of the first classes at Stanford University.

As Hodgkin came to be affected by war, so was Bernal. World War I was ending as he studied mathematics and then natural sciences at Emmanuel College Cambridge. He earned his nickname, Sage, by participating in political discussions with thoughtfulness and intelligence. He later would become a Communist and Marxist. He was such a supporter of the Soviet Union that the World Peace Council, the organization he cofounded with Frederic Joliot-Curie, might have been a bit propagandist in that country's favor, spinning information so that the Soviet Union seemed above criticism. But it also may have encouraged Premier Nikita Khrushchev to stay calmer than he otherwise would have during the Cuban missile crisis.

As Hodgkin did, Bernal also worked under William Bragg, studying crystallography. He invented the X-ray film method, with a rotation camera, and became a lecturer in structural crystallography at Cambridge. His work with steroids, which Hodgkin found so amazing, nearly earned him a Nobel Prize. Now the Society for Social Studies of Science awards an annual John Desmond Bernal Prize.

The Crowfoot Family

No one else in Hodgkin's family worked in X-ray crystallography, but that doesn't mean her parents and sisters didn't inspire and support her along her unique and historic journey. Both of Hodgkin's parents were passionate about education, international work, and research. All four Crowfoot daughters followed their parents' general lead. Elisabeth followed the closest—she went into textile research, same as their mother. Diana worked with her explorer husband Graham

From all angles, Hodgkin was a brilliant scientist.

Rowley on arctic archaeology, anthropology, and geology. Joan was a pioneer in lithic studies, or studies of the stone tools of ancient societies. Interestingly, Dorothy and Joan were also similar in less apparent ways. Both worked diligently but without needing fanfare. They were interested in their research because the challenges and the results were interesting to them, not because they thought there had to be glory in it. As the *Journal of the Council for British Research in the Levant* said of Joan in its obituary of her, her work wasn't flashy, but her dependable success rate and passion laid a basis for generations to come. All of the Crowfoot women quietly, steadily improved the world.

SOMETIMES CRITICISM IS JUST PICKING A SIDE

Dorothy Crowfoot Hodgkin was well respected and well liked throughout her life. Crystallography, which she helped perfect, was recognized even during her time as revolutionary. It would also often provide answers no one was expecting. Critics came from within the crystallography community, too, as these passionate people tried to understand the answers; however, of Hodgkin and her work, there were few if any complaints. Max Perutz, a fellow Nobel-winning chemist, wrote in her obituary in the *Independent*: "She had no enemies, not even among those whose scientific theories she demolished or whose political views she opposed."

For a while, scientists couldn't agree on how the atoms in penicillin linked. One side said it was a thiazolidine-oxazolone structure: two five-membered rings of atoms connected by one bond. The other side thought the beta lactam theory was correct, that one five-membered ring was fused to a four-membered ring. John Cornforth, a contemporary of Hodgkin's, supposedly said that if the beta lactam formula was correct, he'd stop being a chemist and become a mushroom farmer.

Hodgkin took a more open stand. She suggested they let science decide. She was willing to trust scientific experimentation over her own ego to find the truth.

John Cornforth

Artist Maggi Hambling captured Hodgkin's spirit in this oil painting. The piece is part of the National Portrait Gallery's primary collection.

CHAPTER FIVE

FROM GOOGLE DOODLE TO RURAL DIAMOND

A ll scientists and labs leave legacies. When a scientist dies or a lab closes, what becomes of everything that person has done and worked so hard for? Scientists and governing bodies must be thoughtful with knowledge, but there is hope. As you'll see in this chapter, the chain of knowledge, discovery, and human advancement that Dorothy Hodgkin started cannot easily be broken. There are so many strong links now in that chain, all of which help tell the tale of Hodgkin's personal legacy in her field.

CELEBRATING CRYSTALLOGRAPHY

What would Dorothy Hodgkin think if she knew her life and work had been celebrated with a Google Doodle? While she hated the idea of role models, she was happy if people said she'd inspired them or helped them. Plus, she seemed to have a sense of humor and a good outlook on life, so she'd probably smile, knowing she had become a Doodle.

That Google Doodle came out on her birthday in 2014, the Year of Crystallography, as declared by the United Nations. The United Nations

NOT A DAME

When thinking about the awards and honors Dorothy Crowfoot Hodgkin earned, it's hard to think beyond the Nobel Prize, which she won for chemistry in 1964. That's considered one of the top awards in the world, and thus far only four women have received it for chemistry. But other awards Hodgkin received also have lasting effects—and great stories behind the win.

The Order of Merit is the United Kingdom's highest honor. It's considered similar to the Congressional Gold Medal in the United States. There's a twist to the Order of Merit, though—only twenty-four people can hold the honor at any one time. A space opens up only when one of the twenty-four dies. In 1965, Hodgkin became the second woman to receive the Order of Merit. Max Perutz remembered when Hodgkin learned of the honor: an envelope with a return address of Buckingham Palace came in the mail, and she left it sealed. She dreaded the queen wanted to knight her, making her Dame Dorothy. A dame is a female knight. Hodgkin did not like titles, so knighthood wasn't appealing to her. However, when she finally opened the letter, she saw she was receiving the Order of Merit. Hodgkin was pleased, not to mention relieved. Besides, it was a more prestigious title than a knighthood. It's said that there are 150 dames or knights to every person who's been awarded the Order of Merit.

Combine that honor with Hodgkin earning a fellowship of the Royal Society in 1946 and the Royal Society Medal in 1956, and her country has truly shown how much it values her. Today, the Royal Society offers Dorothy Hodgkin fellowships for early-career researchers, ensuring that Hodgkin's value lives on.

resolution stated that its goals for 2014 were, in part, to recognize crystallography as key to understanding the world and to encourage education about crystallography, which impacts everything and could help solve issues of disease and the environment. UNESCO, the United Nations Education, Scientific and Cultural Organization, helped to coordinate celebrations that year. Its director general, Irina Bokova, said crystallography "shaped the history of the twentieth century." Indeed, scientific discoveries and advances due to crystallography have been the reasons for more Nobel Prizes than any other science.

But mere months earlier, the US National Institute of General Medical Sciences (NIGMS) announced that its Protein Structure Initiative (PSI) would end in 2015, fifteen years after it launched. This was a blow to crystallography, which was involved in about 90 percent of the PSI's projects. The PSI had annual funding from the National Institutes of Health of about $70 million. It had a big goal to match its big budget: to solve protein structures, including, in its last five years, to solve those of the particularly challenging membrane proteins. The PSI supplied about 6.5 percent of the protein structures in the Protein Data Bank, where all information about protein, nucleic acid, and complex assembly structures is housed. It also filled a research gap in what most individual investigator grants fund. Such money usually is awarded to scientists studying proteins that are known to have a lot of biomedical interest. But scientists have a knack for wanting to know what they don't even know. The PSI emphasized working toward unknown purposes, just to see what discoveries experimentation could make. This was an institute Dorothy Hodgkin most likely would have been a part of had she been alive to do so.

Despite the upsetting news, the Year of Crystallography continued, bringing to light accomplishments in the field. Among them was

Dorothy Hodgkin. During her lifetime, she inspired and had contact with many future historical figures and scientists, and her legacy lives on today.

MARGARET THATCHER

The first female prime minister of Britain, Margaret Thatcher, was Hodgkin's most well-known student. At the time she worked with Hodgkin, she was Margaret Roberts, hardly known at all.

Politically active in college, leading Oxford's Conservative Association, Thatcher kept her focus on her studies; she earned her chemistry degree and then worked as a research chemist. She started trying to win a political seat only two years after college graduation. During years of trying and failing at that, she married, earned a law degree, and had children. In 1959, a decade after her first political campaign, she was elected to the House of Commons.

Hodgkin likely kept in touch with Thatcher to talk with her about political concerns, although, according to Hodgkin's granddaughter, Katharine Hodgkin, "Dorothy did not have a very high opinion of Thatcher; as a chemist she thought her average; as a politician she deeply disapproved of her." This seems to be backed up by Hodgkin voting against Oxford University giving an honorary doctorate to Thatcher in 1985. Hodgkin felt the prime minister had hurt education with her policies.

JUDITH HOWARD

Judith Howard did not come from a family accomplished in formal education—her father ended his schooling when he was thirteen years old—but she did come from one that placed a great deal of importance

Margaret Thatcher didn't go on to have a career in science after studying under Hodgkin, but she is arguably Hodgkin's most famous student.

Durham University played a key role in Judith Howard's career.

on learning. Howard remembered that her father would call her well into his old age to talk about something he'd read in the newspaper.

Though she read the books that filled her childhood home, she at first focused on dance. Eventually, she outgrew that, literally—one of the leading dance schools said her legs were all wrong—and ended up finding great success in the sciences. In the late 1980s, Judith Howard was invited to apply to lead structural chemistry at Durham University, in the United Kingdom. There she established an internationally renowned lab, was elected a Royal Society fellow, and became the founding director of Durham's Biophysical Sciences Institute. Her work with a Nobel Prize winner, Hodgkin, who was Howard's PhD supervisor, had clearly paid off.

With all her leadership roles, she spends most of her time and energy attending meetings, signing off on paperwork, preparing for assessments, and figuring budgets. Don't call her a nonpracticing scientist, however: "Mind you, I'll make sure I do find some lab time; otherwise I'll go mad."

PAULINE HARRISON

Another of Hodgkin's tutees at Oxford, Pauline Harrison, followed her tutor's fascination with proteins and focused her career on the large iron storage protein ferritin. She successfully determined its structure while giving priority to a research style she considered important: interdisciplinary. She regularly collaborated with clinicians and physicians, as well as with other chemists.

Both of Pauline Harrison's parents were botanists, and her mother had been a trailblazer in her own family by being the only female to attend college. Still, Harrison's father was not comfortable with her interest in chemistry. Fortunately, her mother's support won out.

Harrison has chaired not only the British Biophysical Society, which she cofounded, but also the Sheffield University Fine Arts Society. She focused on her appreciation of painting after retiring from being a professor and researcher, proving that people who practice curiosity in their professions, as scientists do, never stop doing so.

ELEANOR DODSON

Did Eleanor Dodson consider retiring from math after Hodgkin recruited her in the 1960s? How could Dodson reach any higher a success than having a Nobel Prize–winning pioneer recognize her skills and say she needed Dodson in order to do her research well? Of course Dodson could rise even higher—she could become a pioneer in her own field.

She developed analytical tools that make crystallographic techniques accessible to more people, even those outside the field. Because of this work, the Royal Society named her as a fellow in 2003. She cofounded a computing cooperative in 1974 and was one of the main reasons the number of crystallographers studying at York University swelled; everyone wanted to work with her after she joined the faculty in 1976.

Like so many of her female colleagues in math and science, Dodson was mathematician, wife, and mother, all at the same time. She was fortunate in that so many of her employers, from Hodgkin to York University, allowed her work flexibility. For most of her career, she worked on part-time and short-term formal and informal contracts.

ADA YONATH

In the more than one hundred years that the Nobel Committee has been awarding prizes in chemistry, there have been four winners who were female. Of those, two were crystallographers. Dorothy Hodgkin, of course, is one. Ada Yonath, given the award forty-five years after Hodgkin, is the other.

Having educated parents with stable and well-paying jobs can help children become educated for two reasons: if the parents see the value of education, they may wish that for their children, and if the family is financially settled, the children don't have to work or are healthy enough to focus on school. But this is hardly necessary for a child to get a good education.

Ada Yonath was the second female X-ray crystallographer to receive the Nobel Prize, in 2009.

Yonath was raised in poverty. Her parents were not formally educated, and her father was chronically ill. But they put Yonath through a top school, and Yonath fostered her own natural curiosity and intelligence. With humor, Yonath told the Nobel Prize committee that at five years old, she tried to measure the height of her family's covered apartment balcony. She stacked tables and chairs on each other, but she could not manage to reach the ceiling. She did manage to fall from the wobbly pile and break her arm. She noted the experiment would never be completed; new tenants, after her family moved out, remodeled.

Yonath earned degrees and did postdoctoral work in chemistry, biochemistry, and biophysics at prestigious universities in her native Israel as well as in the United States. In 1970, she founded the first—and the only, for ten more years—biological crystallography lab in Israel. Her successes in trying to determine the three-dimensional structure of the ribosome, which is the part of cells that builds protein, will have major practical implications. It could aid in the development of more efficient antibacterial drugs and help in the fight against antibiotic-resistant bacteria.

Decades after five-year-old Yonath's first experiment, Yonath's granddaughter invited her to talk about the ribosome—at her kindergarten. The influence is clear.

RACHEL KLEVIT

A researcher at the University of Washington, Rachel Klevit is the 2016 winner of the Dorothy Crowfoot Hodgkin Award. This is the tenth time the award has been given in recognition of impressive contributions to protein science. Her work has focused on understanding breast cancer and Parkinson's disease. Like Hodgkin, she believes knowing how molecules work together is key to understanding life, which is key to understanding disease, which is key to understanding how to improve and prolong life. She runs her own lab at the university, and she and her students and associates focus on using high-resolution NMR spectroscopy and mass spectrometry, which is an alternative to X-ray crystallography. There are pros and cons to all, depending on the substance and research goals. Klevit also places importance on mentoring younger scientists.

THE SCIENTISTS STUDYING MARS

X-ray diffraction is used everywhere, even outside this world. When trying to figure out if there had ever been life on the planet Mars, scientists used X-ray diffraction on the rocks found on Mars.

Despite what cartoons and movies tell us, scientists were not expecting to find little green people living on Mars. They were hoping to find life forms that are much smaller and, to a degree, much stronger than any human could be. They were wondering if they might find microbes, bacterial life forms. The soil and grit and rocks of Mars's surface are where those microbes would have been.

Archaeologists—like so many members of Hodgkin's family have been, including Hodgkin herself—dig in the ground for objects left behind by people who lived a long time ago. Studying those objects tells us about the people who made, used, and discarded those objects. What did they need to live? What resources did they have available to them? Scientists studying Mars are doing the same thing regarding microbes. But what microbes leave behind is too small to dig up with a trowel and clean with a brush, as archaeologists do items left by humans. So scientists turn to technology, to powerful X-rays.

They collect a nice sample from Mars's surface. In this pile will be a wide variety of types and sizes of dirt and rock. The scientists shoot a

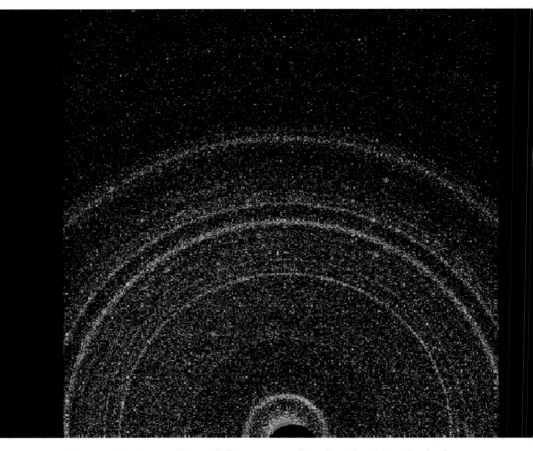

In 2012, scientists used X-ray diffraction to analyze the soil on Mars, for the first time identifying without doubt that planet's soil makeup. They found that sample to be similar to volcanic soil in Hawaii.

Dorothy Hodgkin: Biochemist and Discoverer of Protein Crystallography

concentrated X-ray beam at the dirt. The light diffracts, or shoots out in different directions, just as it did for Hodgkin and her colleagues, who aimed X-ray beams at protein crystals. And just as Hodgkin captured a photograph from this, of dots, the Mars scientists capture a photograph of their work. Their images show up as rings, called Debye Rings, and not as individual dots, but the scientists proceed as Hodgkin did. They use Bragg's law to calculate how big the spaces are between layers of atoms. Now they know what type of minerals they're looking at.

One of the most thrilling discoveries scientists have made is that there is riverbed clay on Mars. X-ray diffraction told them that they were looking at the type of clay that can only form under certain conditions—not too acidic, not too salty. In other words, this clay formed near water that would have been perfectly drinkable by humans. There may have been life, as we understand it, on Mars.

THE SCIENTISTS USING DIAMOND LIGHT SOURCE

Diamond is a nonprofit organization impressive in both size and scope of mission, which is to study basically everything, as Hodgkin and her peers in crystallography did. The people who run it are not shy about expressing the debt fit owes Hodgkin. The scientific research organization celebrated International Women's Day on March 8, 2015, by focusing on Hodgkin. It tweeted a link to an article describing how her work led directly to Diamond's current experiments. Without Hodgkin, Diamond very well might not have existed.

Diamond is based in London. It is funded by the government of the United Kingdom, via the Science and Technology Council, and the Wellcome Trust, a charity that supports research into the health of humans and other animals. The facility is free to scientists who work

Dorothy Hodgkin: Biochemist and Discoverer of Protein Crystallography

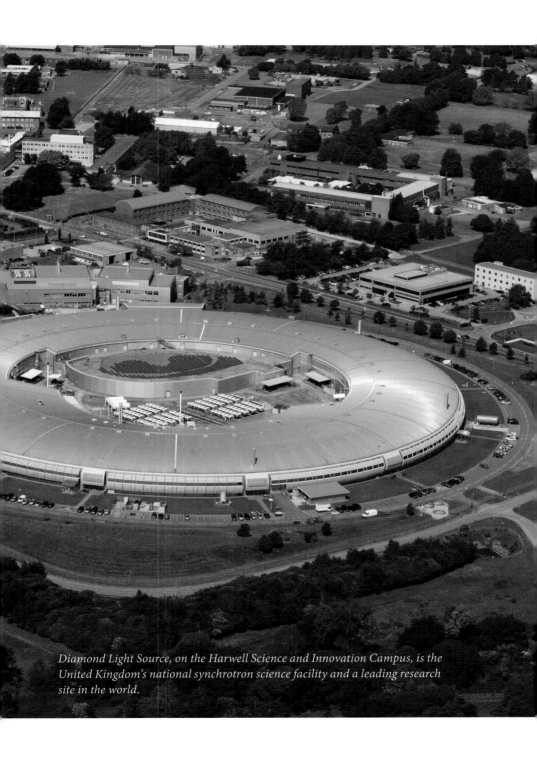

Diamond Light Source, on the Harwell Science and Innovation Campus, is the United Kingdom's national synchrotron science facility and a leading research site in the world.

THE NEXT GENERATION OF HODGKIN: JENNY PICKWORTH GLUSKER

The number of similarities between Dorothy Crowfoot Hodgkin and her student Jenny Pickworth Glusker is fascinating. Both are British, and both grew up with parents who encouraged their daughters' studies. As Hodgkin's interest in chemistry started with a book, so did Glusker's. From one of her mother's medical books, she learned how mixing pills could cause a bad reaction in patients. She then got a chemistry set. With it she made "wonderfully colored solutions and evil-smelling products."

Hodgkin interviewed Glusker for admission to Somerville and then became her tutor. They met one-on-one every week. Though Hodgkin did not like the term "role model," Glusker saw her as one. She was a successful chemist, and she had a husband and kids. Glusker had decided she would not leave her own career if she ever had children.

Eventually, Glusker and her chemist husband looked for jobs in the United States. (Like Hodgkin, Glusker met her husband while in school.) It was an uphill battle, in large part because Glusker was a woman. You might think if a woman had a doctorate in chemistry, how could she be denied a great job? Easy: companies often house their own libraries, and they'd hire women as librarians. If they had children, it didn't matter how many degrees they had. Finally, two chemical companies in Philadelphia accepted Glusker and her husband. Glusker wrote to Hodgkin for a letter of recommendation. Hodgkin's reply was that Glusker's talents belonged somewhere with a greater purpose. She suggested Glusker apply at the Institute for Cancer Research (ICR) in Philadelphia.

Glusker worked at ICR her whole career. She studied chemical carcinogens and antitumor agents. By learning their structures, she and her colleagues could understand how they react with the body. Like Hodgkin, Glusker educated others and led professional organizations; while Hodgkin was president of the International Union of Crystallography, Glusker was president of the American Crystallographic Association.

in schools and in corporations and who pass a rigorous application process. They also must promise to put the results of their research in the public domain. That is, they won't own it—anyone can study it and make use of it.

Diamond Light Source is the technology everyone who visits Diamond wants to use. It's the United Kingdom's synchrotron, a powerful source of X-rays that are ten billion times brighter than the sun. It works like a giant microscope, allowing us to learn about everything from fossils to viruses. It's sort of the next generation of the X-ray tube that Hodgkin used, as did all her colleagues, from the discovery of X-rays in the late 1800s until about 1960. While it took Hodgkin more than thirty years to figure out insulin's atomic structure, it would take a scientist using Diamond Light Source one hour.

The reason for the leap in time is that technology has advanced a great deal. Scientists today are able to use ever-tinier crystals because they have access to more intense X-rays that produce higher-resolution images than scientists had back in Hodgkin's day. Computers crunch data much more quickly and accurately than they did during that time, too. Diamond also mentions the breakthrough scientists made when they started freezing protein crystals, which reduces the amount of damage an X-ray can do to a crystal. Helen Megaw, Hodgkin's contemporary, was freezing crystals a long time ago—like Diamond scientists, Hodgkin herself benefitted from the technique of freezing crystals, but she did so directly because of another female scientist's smarts!

In 1980, the first synchrotron radiation source (SRS) was built. Five years later, X-ray diffraction allowed scientists to solve the structures of two human viruses: polio and the common cold. In 1997, John Walker was the first person to win a Nobel Prize (in chemistry) for work driven by synchrotron rays. More such awards, for other scientists working on different problems, quickly followed: Nobel Prizes were awarded in 2003 and in 2006 for work done with synchrotrons. Then in 2009, DNA came back into the story. Its discovery happened because of X-ray diffraction. Sixty years later, another advancement in the understanding of DNA happened because advancements in technology allowed for synchrotron radiation. Venkatraman Ramakrishnan, Thomas A. Steitz, and Ada Yonath studied ribosome's structure and function using this tool.

JACK DUNITZ

Jack Dunitz was one of Hodgkin's postdoctoral researchers, meaning he helped her in her lab after he earned his PhD. Together, they worked on some of the most complex structures ever to be investigated with X-ray crystallography. He was with Hodgkin when she saw the not-yet-published DNA structure. In addition to Oxford, he worked at the California Institute of Technology (Caltech), the NIH Institute of Mental Health, the Royal Institution in London, and the Swiss Federal Institute of Technology.

Dunitz studied in Glasgow, Scotland, where he had been born. As so many students and researchers were, he was affected by war. World War II made him pack his undergraduate work into three years. Another hallmark of many successful researchers: Dunitz was a self-starter; with his doctoral supervisor busy with administrative duties, Dunitz had to find his own learning opportunities. That's how he found X-ray crystallography.

He would say the reverse actually happened, that crystallography chose him, as going into the sciences at all did: "It just happened, as in a dream. In a dream, you don't do things, things happen to you." As

Hodgkin had, Dunitz had a casualness about him. He was appointed to high positions and won awards for his work in crystallography, but he was always just a regular person. He swore that at Caltech he was better known for the cabaret shows he put on with a biologist colleague than for his scientific contributions.

HODGKIN'S FAMILY: THE NEXT GENERATIONS

Just as it was important to mention the family Dorothy Hodgkin grew up with as people who influenced her, it's important to mention some of the family members who came after her. Even if they didn't follow exactly in her professional footsteps, they surely were influenced by her. Her intelligence, casual humility, curiosity, determination, and good humor provided a setting in which they could be and do what they wanted to be and do.

All three of her children went on to academic or research careers. Among other things, Luke has been a professor of mathematics at King's College London. Elizabeth has been a human rights researcher for Amnesty International, earning a PhD in history, and has edited a collection of her father's letters. Toby has worked in agrobiodiversity research for the Commission on Genetic Resources for Food and Agriculture, an organization that facilitates countries peacefully debating questions and issues of agriculture production that otherwise could lead to political arguments. In the next generation of Hodgkin's family, there are, among others, a historian, an astronomer, and an anthropologist.

"I HAVE SEEN THE FUTURE, AND IT IS VERY MUCH LIKE THE PRESENT, ONLY LONGER"

It's possible that Dorothy's legacy will be both very much what she herself experienced in her work and very much what she might have expected the work to turn into. Crystallography may very well continue as it has been going, just stronger, faster, with more and more advanced technology. Of course, as Nils Bohr, who won a Nobel Prize in Physics, said, it's difficult to predict the future. Dorothy said something like that, too. Crystallography allows for exploration, experimentation, surprises under the surface just waiting to be discovered. As advancements in the field occur, the field will actually start to look quite a bit different than it used to. Consider how different Hodgkin's work looked from Emil Fischer's. Are both still crystallography? Yes and no. Will the crystallography of tomorrow seem more "no" than "yes" if advancements start taking away previous definitions of crystallography—for example, what if improved lasers remove the need for substances to be purified into crystals?

SOME IMPORTANT PUBLICATIONS

Dorothy Hodgkin never wrote a book on crystallography. However, she contributed in other ways, by writing and cowriting hundreds of papers on the subject. The National Cataloguing Unit for the Archives of Contemporary Scientists compiled a catalog of Hodgkin's papers. In 1991, Hodgkin gave permission for the papers to be catalogued and kept in the Bodleian Library of Oxford. The CWP, the Contributions of 20th Century Women to Physics archive at the University of California, Los Angeles, suggests the following among Hodgkin's most important

Hodgkin has been celebrated twice on British postage stamps. This is the first, released as part of the Women of Achievement issue in 1996.

papers: "The X-ray Analysis of Complicated Molecules"; "The Crystal Structure of Cholesteryl Iodide"; "X-ray Crystallographic Investigation of the Structure of Penicillin,"; and "Atomic Positions in Rhombohedral 2-zinc Insulin Crystals."

CONCLUSION

Researching the life and times of Hodgkin, her colleagues, and the scientists who came before and after her reveals so many common threads. Hodgkin was curious and grounded, kind and showing good humor, a self-starting visionary who recognized the importance of peace and justice. The state of the home (family opinion, involvement, and experience) and the state of the world (wars and economics) played big roles in her life. Being able to balance home and work lives was also important. And these points were raised time and time again in other scientists' biographies. It's exciting to see how lineages are built, how paths and people cross, reflect each other, and diverge into tracks that progress the bigger scientific field, and humanity overall.

CHRONOLOGY

1859	Alfred Baring Garrod defines rheumatoid arthritis.
1895	Wilhelm Röntgen discovers X-rays.
1910	Dorothy Crowfoot is born in Cairo, Egypt, to British parents.
1911	Triangle Shirtwaist Factory Fire kills 146 people, many of them under age twenty.
1914	Great Britain enters World War I.
1917	The United States enters World War I, and the Selective Service Act (passing into law on May 18, 1917) introduces the draft.
1920	Hodgkin becomes interested in chemistry and crystals. Earns masters degree in mathematics.
1921–1928	Hodgkin studies at Sir John Leman School, Beccles, England.
1925	Hodgkin reads her first book on crystallography, *Concerning the Nature of Things,* by W. H. Bragg.

1928	Alexander Fleming discovers penicillin.
1928–1932	Hodgkin attends Somerville College at Oxford University. For a brief time, she studies both archaeology and chemistry, but a course in X-ray crystallography settles her focus.
1932	Hodgkin graduates Somerville College with a chemistry degree.
1932–1934	Hodgkin studies with J. D. Bernal at Cambridge University.
1934	Hodgkin is diagnosed with rheumatoid arthritis; Hodgkin and Bernal photograph pepsin with X-rays, launching protein crystallography.
1934–1935	Hodgkin is a research fellow at Somerville College, Oxford.
1935–1955	Hodgkin is an official fellow and tutor at Somerville College.
1936	Hodgkin successfully photographs insulin with X-rays.
1936–1939	The Arab uprising happens in Palestine.

1937	Hodgkin is awarded her Cambridge PhD and marries Dr. Thomas Hodgkin, an expert in African affairs.
1938	Hodgkin and Thomas's first child, Luke, is born.
1939	Great Britain enters World War II.
1940	Howard Florey and Ernst Chain make groundbreaking discovery about penicillin.
1941	The United States enters World War II; Hodgkin and Thomas's second child, Elizabeth, is born.
1941–1942	Hodgkin determines the structure of cholesteryl iodide by X-ray diffraction.
1942–1949	Using X-ray diffraction, Hodgkin studies, determines, and publishes about the structure of penicillin.
1944	Oxford's Department of Mineralogy and Crystallography is divided, and Hodgkin stays with the subdepartment of Chemical Crystallography.
1945	Hodgkin determines penicillin's structure; World War II ends.

1946	Hodgkin helps with the initial meetings in the creation of the International Union of Crystallography; Hodgkin's and Thomas's third child, Toby, is born.
1946–1956	Hodgkin is an Oxford lecturer and demonstrator.
1947	Hodgkin is awarded a fellowship of the Royal Society because of her work with penicillin.
1948	Vitamin B12 is isolated, and Hodgkin begins work on it.
1955	Hodgkin takes the first X-ray diffraction photographs of vitamin B12; the Russell-Einstein Manifesto is published.
1956	Hodgkin determines the structure of B12 (see also 1961); is awarded the Royal Medal and becomes a foreign member of the Royal Netherlands Academy of Sciences. She also becomes an Oxford University reader in X-ray crystallography.
1958	Hodgkin is made a member of the American Academy of Arts and Sciences.
1960–1977	Hodgkin works as Wolfson Research Professor of the Royal Society.

1961	The structure that was determined in 1956 was later understood to not be the naturally active vitamin. The complete structure was finalized in 1961.
1964	Hodgkin wins the Nobel Prize for Chemistry for her work on vitamin B12.
1965	Queen Elizabeth II presents Hodgkin with the Order of Merit.
1969	Hodgkin calculates the three-dimensional structure of the protein insulin, thirty-four years after she first successfully photographed it.
1971–1988	Hodgkin serves as chancellor of Bristol University.
1972	Hodgkin is the Bakerian Lecturer at the National Academy of Sciences in the United States.
1972–1975	Hodgkin is president of the International Union of Crystallography.
1975–1988	Hodgkin is president of the Pugwash Conference on Science and World Affairs.
1976	Hodgkin is given the Copley Medal from the Royal Society of London; is made a member of the USSR Academy of Sciences.
1977–1978	Hodgkin is president of the British Association for the Advancement of Science.

1978	Hodgkin is awarded the Longstaff Medal from the British Association for the Advancement of Sciences.
1982	Hodgkin receives the Mikhail Lomonosov Gold Medal from the Soviet Academy of Sciences.
1984	Hodgkin wins the Dimitrov Prize.
1987	Hodgkin wins the Lenin Peace Prize.
1994	Dorothy Hodgkin dies after a stroke, at her home in Shipston-on-Stour, England.

GLOSSARY

atom The smallest particle of a substance.

atomic structure The organization of atoms.

chemistry The study of matter and the changes it experiences.

cross-disciplinary Relating to more than one branch of knowledge.

crystallography The study of atomic and molecular structures.

diffraction pattern Shows in what directions the X-ray scattered after being sent through a crystal.

epimerization A chemical process affecting the chiral centers, tetrahedral atoms (usually carbons), in a molecule.

hypothesis An idea or theory not yet proven.

molecular structure The organization of molecules.

oxidation A chemical reaction by which an atom loses an electron.

Patterson map Shows the vectors between heavy atoms.

protein crystallography The study of the structure of proteins.

rheumatoid arthritis A disease of the joints that causes increasing pain over time.

synthesize Make something complex by combining simpler substances.

X-ray crystallography The study of a substance's structure by use of X-ray diffraction.

X-ray tube A device for generating X-rays.

FURTHER INFORMATION

BOOKS

Maddox, Brenda. *Rosalind Franklin: The Dark Lady of DNA*.
London, UK: HarperCollins Publishers, 2002.

Senechal, Marjorie. *I Died for Beauty: Dorothy Wrinch and the
Cultures of Science*. Oxford, UK: Oxford University Press, 2012.

WEBSITE

Nature Milestones: Crystallography

http://www.nature.com/milestones/milecrystal/index.html

Nature Milestones highlight achievements in scientific fields. In this
one, you can read articles on twenty-five different events or topics in
crystallography's history and view a timeline of milestones.

VIDEOS

BBC: An Eye for Pattern: The Letters of Dorothy Hodgkin

http://www.bbc.co.uk/programmes/b04lc3gt

In this five-part BBC Radio series, Dorothy's biographer, Georgina
Ferry, narrates letters from and to Dorothy. This is a great way to
hear the warm, human side of sharp, factual science.

Ri Channel: A Case of Crystal Clarity

http://richannel.org/a-case-of-crystal-clarity

An animated critter experiences X-ray crystallography firsthand as he's isolated, crystallized, X-rayed, and analyzed. The little green fellow survives, and the viewer of this short animation understands crystallography a bit better.

The Royal Institution

http://richannel.org

This London-based nonprofit helps people understand science through entertaining educational lectures and videos.

The Royal Institution

"Celebrating Crystallography—An Animated Adventure"

https://www.youtube.com/watch?v=uqQlwYv8VQI

This short animated explanation and history of crystallography is fun and informative to watch.

BIBLIOGRAPHY

"A Science Odyssey: People and Discoveries: Dorothy Hodgkin 1910–1994." PBS.org. Accessed May 26, 2016. http://www.pbs.org/wgbh/aso/databank/entries/bmhodg.html.

American Crystallographic Association. "Careers in Crystallography: Exploring the Structure of Matter." Accessed May 24, 2016. http://www.amercrystalassn.org/content/pages/main-careers.

Apotheker, Jan, and Livia Simon Sarkadi. *European Women in Chemistry*. Hoboken, NJ: John Wiley and Sons, 2011.

Ashton, Kevin. *How to Fly a Horse: The Secret History of Creation, Invention, and Discovery*. New York: Knopf Doubleday Publishing Group, 2015.

"A Bittersweet Celebration of Crystallography." *Nature*. May 29, 2014. http://www.nature.com/nmeth/journal/v11/n6/full/nmeth.2995.html.

Chemical Heritage Foundation. "Dorothy Crowfoot Hodgkin." Accessed May 24, 2016. http://www.chemheritage.org/discover/online-resources/chemistry-in-history/themes/molecular-synthesis-structure-and-bonding/hodgkin.aspx.

Cohen, Linda Juliana. "Dr. Dorothy Crowfoot Hodgkin: Chemist, Crystallographer, Humanitarian." Almaz.com. Accessed May 26, 2016. http://www.almaz.com/nobel/chemistry/dch.html.

"Crystallography." American Chemical Society. Last accessed May
27, 2016. http://www.acs.org/content/acs/en/careers/college-to-
career/chemistry-careers/cystallography.html.

Curry, Stephen. "Seeing Things in a Different Light: How X-Ray
Crystallography Revealed the Structure of Everything."
Filmed October 25, 2013. Crystallography Collection, The
Royal Institution Channel, 1:02:47. https://www.youtube.com/
watch?v=gBxZVF3s4cU.

Del Giudice, Marguerite. "Why It's Crucial to Get More Women
into Science." Last updated January 21, 2015. http://news.
nationalgeographic.com/news/2014/11/141107-gender-studies-
women-scientific-research-feminist/.

Dodson, Guy. Interview with Dorothy Crowfoot Hodgkin, 1990.
Web of Stories. Posted October 2, 2009. http://www.webofstories.
com/play/dorothy.hodgkin/1 "Dorothy Hodgkin—A Lifetime
of Scientific Endeavor: Celebrating the Mother of Structural
Biology." Diamond. Accessed May 31, 2016. http://www.diamond.
ac.uk/Home/News/LatestNews/28_03_14.html.

Ferry, Georgina. *Dorothy Hodgkin: A Life*. London, UK:
Bloomsbury Academic, 2014.

———. "Dorothy Crowfoot Hodgkin." Trowelblazers.
http://trowelblazers.com/dorothy-crowfoot-hodgkin.

———. "History: Women in Crystallography." *Nature*. January 29,
2014. http://www.nature.com/news/history-women-in-
crystallography-1.14588.

"Georgina Ferry on X-Ray Crystallography." Filmed 2008. Wellcome Collection, Ri Channel, 6:53. http://richannel.org/georgina-ferry-on-x-ray-crystallography.

Hodgkin, Dorothy Crowfoot. "The X-Ray Analysis of Complicated Molecules." Nobel Lecture (December 11, 1964). http://www.nobelprize.org/nobel_prizes/chemistry/laureates/1964/hodgkin-lecture.pdf.

Hodgkin, Katharine. "Thatcher and Hodgkin: A Personal and Political Chemistry." *The Guardian*. August 24, 2014. https://www.theguardian.com/science/political-science/2014/aug/24/thatcher-and-hodgkin-a-personal-and-political-chemistry.

"How Do X-Rays Work?" The National Institute of Biomedical Imaging and Bioengineering, National Institutes of Health, 1:29. Posted November 26, 2014. https://www.youtube.com/watch?v=hTz_rGP4v9Y.

"Mars Diffracts! X-ray Crystallography and Space Exploration." The Royal Institution, 11:43. Posted April 17, 2014. https://www.youtube.com/watch?v=lr_PDXyNu1E.

Mueck, Leonie. "Imagine a Crystal's Inner Life." Nature. July 17, 2014. http://www.nature.com/milestones/milecrystal/full/milecrystal01.html.

Newman, Paul. "Catalogue of the Papers and Correspondence of Dorothy Mary Crowfoot Hodgkin, 1828–1993: Peace and Humanitarian Interests." Bodleian Library, University of Oxford, 1994, 2012. http://www.bodley.ox.ac.uk/dept/scwmss/wmss/online/modern/hodgkin/hodgkin-main.html.

Nobelprize.org. "Banquet Speech." Accessed May 26, 2016. http://
www.nobelprize.org/nobel_prizes/chemistry/laureates/1964/
hodgkin-speech.html.

————. "Dorothy Crowfoot Hodgkin—Biographical." Accessed
May 24, 2016. http://www.nobelprize.org/nobel_prizes/
chemistry/laureates/1964/hodgkin-bio.html.

Perutz, Max. "Obituary: Professor Dorothy Hodgkin." *Independent*.
July 31, 1994. http://www.independent.co.uk/news/people/
obituary-professor-dorothy-hodgkin-1373624.html.

Rayner-Canham, Marelene F., and Geoffrey Rayner-Canham.
*Chemistry Was Their Life: Pioneering British Women Chemists,
1880–1949*. London: Imperial College "2014 Is the International
Year of Crystallography." International Council for Science.
Accessed May 27, 2016. http://www.icsu.org/news-centre/news/
top-news/2014-is-the-international-year-of-crystallography.

"Understanding Crystallography—Part 1: From Proteins to
Crystals." The Royal Institution, 7:47. Posted April 2, 2014.
https://youtu.be/gLsC4wlrR2A.

"Understanding Crystallography—Part 2: From Crystals to
Diamond." The Royal Institution, 11:43. Posted April 10, 2014.
https://www.youtube.com/watch?v=WJKvDUo3KRk.

Vijayan, M. "An Outstanding Scientist and Great Humanist: An
Obituary of Dorothy Crowfoot Hodgkin." International Union
of Crystallography. Accessed May 26, 2016. http://www.iucr.
org/people/crystallographers/an-obituary-of-dorothy-crowfoot-
hodgkin.

INDEX

Nobel Prize, 5, 7, 13, 26, 31–32, 34, **36,** 38, 52, 54, 80–82, 88–89, 93–94, 96, 104–105, 107

Oxford University, 15, 62, 72, 75, 90
oxidation, 51

Patterson map, 16
Pauling, Linus, 38, 75
peace, work for, 6, 20, 29–31, 35, 37–38, 73, 109
penicillin, 6, **17,** 31–32, 34–35, 49, 55–56, 63, 81, 84, 109
pepsin, 16, 20, 33, 78
Perutz, Max, 26, 34, 38, 40, 44, 61, 75–76, **77,** 84, 88
PhD, 9, 24, 69, 75, 80, 93, 105–106
Philpot, John, 33
Porter, Polly, 24, 62–63
protein crystallography, 16, 46
protein strands, 17
proteins, 5, 16–17, 25, 33, 44, 46, 51, 75, 89, 93
Pugwash movement, 6, 35

rheumatoid arthritis, 16
ribosome, 96, 105
Rogers-Low, Barbara, 81
role models, 69, 72, 87, 102
Röntgen, Wilhelm, 52, 56, 58

Somerville College, 15, 21, 23–24, 26, 72–73, 102
Sudan, 10–12, 15
synchrotron, 80, 104–105
synthesize, 34, 41, 51

Thatcher, Margaret, 90, **91**

Vietnam War, 30
Vietnam, involvement with, 20, 29–30
viruses, 5, 20, 38, 44, 51, 79, 104
vitamin B12, 6, 34, 41, 70
von Laue, Max, 52, 56, 58, 60–61

Watson, James, 38, 40, 70–71, 79
Wilkins, Maurice, 38, 40, 70
women in the workforce, 25

ABOUT THE AUTHOR

Kristin Thiel lives in Portland, Oregon, where she is a writer and editor of books, articles, and documents for businesses. She has worked on many of the books in the So, You Want to Be A... series, which offers career guidance for kids. She's the lead writer on a report for her city about funding for high school dropout prevention. Thiel has judged YA book contests and helped start a Kids Voting USA affiliate. She has been a substitute teacher in grades K–12 and managed before-school and afterschool literacy programs for AmeriCorps VISTA. Thiel's own scientific experiments include finding the best angles to bend her arm for comfortable snuggling for both her and her cat.